FOCUSING

LEARN FROM THE MASTERS

FOCUSING

LEARN FROM THE MASTERS

FOUR TRAINING MANUALS

Compiled and Edited By

LUCINDA GRAY, PH.D.

NEW BUDDHA BOOKS

FOCUSING - LEARN FROM THE MASTERS
A New Buddha Book

Originally Published as:
Focusing Training in an Urban High School
Teaching the Teachers Focusing
A Manual and Anthology of Writings
Created For
A Focusing Training Intervention in Los Angeles Spring 2009
Compiled and Edited By
Lucinda Gray, Ph.D. and Diana Marder, Ph.D.
First Edition 2009
Copyright© 2009 by Lucinda Gray, Ph.D.
All rights reserved.

ISBN-13: 978-0615765211 (New Buddha Books)

ISBN-10: 0615765211

CONTENTS

INTRODUCTION

This collection represents some of the very best available writing on Focusing from the most esteemed teachers. It was first developed by me in collaboration with Dr. Diana Marder for use in our school project in Los Angeles in the spring of 2009. The project involved Focusing training for the teachers in an urban high school. None of the teachers had been exposed to Focusing prior to the program, so we designed the anthology to progressively introduce the concepts and practice of Focusing. We included experiential practice in each of the four manuals, each of which accompanied a 2.5 hour workshop. We were allowed only ten hours of teacher time for the training, so we were surprised and thrilled to find that the program had a positive effect on students: specifically on absenteeism, drop-out rate and grades.

Since the first publication of this anthology I have received requests from Focusing trainers and Coordinators around the world who wish to use these four manuals for teaching Focusing to a general audience of students and trainers. In response to this need my husband David Truslow agreed to spend the time to re-format the book into this nice 6x9 version, so that we could make it available at a greatly reduced price. Since the collection will be used as a general training aid, not just in an educational setting, I made the decision to re-order the articles in a way that I think maximizes their effectiveness. I moved the materials about educational issues to the final section of the book, leaving the more general articles in the first three parts of the collection. I suggest you read the articles on education even if you are not a teacher or parent. They are fascinating, and they show the amazing ways that Focusing can benefit students. At the end of section four you will find two great articles on checking in with yourself, and helping someone else with a check in. They are useful for all of us.

After thirty years of learning and teaching Focusing, and practicing Focusing Oriented Psychotherapy, I still find it to be the most effective change process I have ever encountered. It has changed and enriched my life beyond measure. As I re-read these articles I was again impressed and inspired by the quality of the work presented here. I am grateful to all the authors for their brilliant contributions to this collection.

Lucinda Gray Ph.D.
Santa Ana, Costa Rica
March 1, 2013

FOCUSING

LEARN FROM THE MASTERS

TRAINING MANUAL I

Essential Principals of Focusing
Lucinda Gray, Ph.D.

Focusing was developed at the University of Chicago, by Eugene Gendlin in the 1960s, based on research on what makes therapy work; the nature of the change process itself. Focusing is a generic change process; a specific method for accessing the deepest inner truth that we all carry inside. Gendlin's first paper on Focusing was published in the Journal of Psychotherapy, Theory, Research and Practice in 1969. Focusing has been evolving over the past 40 years and has become a primary tool for therapists: Focusing Oriented Psychotherapy. Now it is taught in graduate training programs all over the world.

Focusing is based on the idea that experiencing is an ongoing bodily felt process from which meaning evolves. Change is a body experience. Lasting change can only occur when we have a bodily experience of difference. When a feeling is correctly symbolized through a word, phrase or image, the body recognizes the change, and we feel a sense of relief inside. This is our own inner truth, validated by body experience. Focusing teaches specific steps that enable us to access and symbolize feelings so that the deeper knowing that they carry can come to awareness.

Feelings are the language the body uses to convey information. Pain, tightness or anxiety, often signals something within you that wants to be known. With Focusing you can learn how to gently receive the information within. You can

13

learn to connect with the place deep inside where you already know what is right for you.

Focusing is multidimensional. By joining right and left brain functions, focusing taps into a whole new level of consciousness. It makes the intuitive function available to us on an ongoing basis. Focusing can be used to work with emotional issues, personal problems and as a psychotherapeutic tool. It is also a powerful tool for problem solving, theory building (TAE) and creative process.

What Makes Focusing Work?
The Focusing Matrix

1) Let go of trying to make something happen or fix something.

2) Begin with a blameless, nonjudgmental acceptance of feelings and inner experience. Your body carries a deep knowing of who you are and what might fit for you.

3) Get the idea that some improvement in your inner experience is actually possible, that change is possible.

4) Treat your feelings as you would treat a guest in your house, sitting with them and attending to them.

5) Realize that you can feel better even without having an answer for an issue you might be working on.

6) Get the idea that words and images can come directly from body experience.

7) Get the idea that action steps can come from bodily felt experience.

The Focusing Matrix is a conceptual framework; a philosophical position essential for Focusing to work. Focusing teaches a way of being with feelings, respecting and making friends with them in a neutral way; holding a gentle nonjudgmental curiosity toward whatever you find inside. This welcoming curiosity is an essential support to the change process. Nothing changes in us when it is rejected. Only by allowing whatever feeling comes up, even if we don't like it, can we reach a peaceful and clear space.

Focusing means letting go of trying to make anything happen or to fix any problem you have and simply paying attention to whatever you might be carrying now. You can trust your process. Change is the nature of the human organism. When feelings are acknowledged, named and respected they naturally change. Only by pushing our feelings away can we stay stuck. Acknowledging the feeling implies that it is important and deserves our attention. Here I am using the term acknowledging to describe a special quality of attention. It is a benign and accepting attention we give to our inner experience. We see it as valuable information, always implying a much larger meaning.

Focusing works when you can hold whatever you find inside in a caring loving presence. It works when you trust your own inner process and give it time. Simply stay with the sensation/feeling until words or images emerge and it begins to change on its own.

Bibliography

Gendlin, E.T. (1962). *Experience in the Creation of Meaning*, New York: McMillan

Gendlin, E.T. (1973). Experiential Psychotherapy in Corsini (Ed.) *Current Psychotherapies*. Itasca: F.E. Peacock

Gendlin, E.T. (1981). *Focusing*. New York: Bantam Books

Gendlin, E.T. (1991). On Emotion in Therapy" in Safran and Greenberg (Eds.) *Emotion, Therapy, and Change*. New York; Guilford, pp. 255-279.

Gendlin, E.T. (1996). *Focusing-Oriented Psychotherapy*. New York: Guilford

Hendricks, Marion. (2002) Research Basis of Focusing-Oriented/ Experiential Therapy, in Cain, D. and Seeman, J. (Eds.) *Handbook of Research and Practice in Humanistic Psychotherapies*. APA

Clearing a Space: The First Step of Focusing

As developed by Eugene Gendlin, Ph.D.
Amended by Dianna Marder, Ph.D.

1. When you are ready, you might want to close your eyes, getting comfortable in your chair, letting yourself take a few slow breaths, bringing your attention to your arms, your legs, and finally to the center of your body, your insides. Ask yourself, "What's in the way of feeling fine right now?" Whatever comes, notice how it feels in your body.

2. Now see if there is a word, a phrase, or an image that captures the quality of how the concern feels in your body. Say the word, phrase, or image back to yourself, and check to see if it fits the sense you have there.

3. Now give this concern your accepting, friendly attention for a few moments; just say "Yes, that's there". Now put it aside for a while by imagining that you are placing it *outside of your body*, like putting down a heavy load. Sometimes it helps to imagine that you're sitting on a park bench, and each concern can be wrapped up like a package, and placed on the park bench next to you. Notice if you feel a little lighter or clearer inside without *that* one.*

4. Now again, bring your attention inside and asking, "Except for that, am I feeling fine?" Wait and see if something else wants your attention next.** If so, repeat steps 2-4. Continue until nothing else comes up.

5. Now, in addition to those issues and concerns, most of us have a background sense – always feeling a little anxious, or sad, or harried, or tense. So, see if there's a background sense that's there today for you, and place that out as well.

6. Now bringing your attention back inside your body, notice how it feels in your body now that these issues have been placed aside. See if there is a clearer space there, and notice what that is like for you. Welcome this space and seeing if a word or an image captures how it feels there, in the clear or clearer space.

7. If you have not found a clear space, you might ask: "How would I like to feel right now?" See if you can let an answer come from your body, and find a word or phrase that fits that. Spend a bit of time sensing what that would be like.

If none of these works, you may have to Focus on the issue for a little while before it will move.

*If you do not feel lighter, you can try some other ways of putting it aside. (a) Imagine the feeling stays there but *you* move away from *it.* (b) Move it far, far away-hundreds of miles if necessary. (c) Imagine that the problem has been magically solved.

**You do not have to deal with all your problems, only what's with you *right now.*

Three Key Aspects of Focusing

Ann Weiser Cornell, Ph.D.
Appeared in The Focusing Connection, March 1998

There are three key qualities or aspects which set Focusing apart from any other method of inner awareness and personal growth. The first is something called the "felt sense." The second is a special quality of engaged, accepting inner attention. And the third is a radical philosophy of what facilitates change. Let's take these one by one.

The Focusing process involves coming into the body and finding there a special kind of body sensation called a "felt sense." Eugene Gendlin was the first person to name and point to a felt sense, even though human beings have been having felt senses as long as they've been human. A felt sense, to put it simply, is a body sensation that has meaning. You've certainly been aware of a felt sense at some time in your life, and possibly you feel them often.

Imagine being on the phone with someone you love who is far away, and you really miss that person, and you just found out in this phone call that you're not going to be seeing them soon. You get off the phone, and you feel a heaviness in your chest, perhaps around the heart area. Or let's say you're sitting in a room full of people and each person is going to take a turn to speak, and as the turn comes closer and closer to you, you feel a tightness in your stomach, like a spring winding tighter and tighter. Or let's say you're taking a walk on a beautiful fresh morning, just after a rain, and you come over a hill, and there in the air in front of you is a perfect rainbow, both sides touching the ground, and as you stand there and gaze at it you feel your chest welling with an expansive flowing, warm feeling. These are all felt senses.

If you're operating purely with emotions, then fear is fear. It's just fear, no more. But if you're operating on the felt sense level, you can sense that this fear, the one you're feeling right now, is different from the fear you felt yesterday. Maybe yesterday's fear was like a cold rock in the stomach, and today's fear is like a pulling back, withdrawing. As you stay with today's fear, you start to sense something like a shy creature pulled back into a cave. You get the feeling that if you sit with it long enough; you might even find out the real reason that it is so scared. A felt sense is often subtle, and as you pay attention to it you discover that it is intricate. It has more to it. We have a vocabulary of emotions that we feel over and over again, but every felt sense is different. You can, however, start with an emotion, and then feel the felt sense of it, as you are feeling it in your body right now.

Felt sensing is not something that other methods teach. There is no one else, outside of Focusing, who is talking about this dimension of experience which is not emotion and not thought, which is subtle yet concretely felt, absolutely physically real. Felt sensing is one of the things that makes it Focusing.

The second key aspect of Focusing is a special quality of engaged accepting inner attention.

In the Focusing process, after you are aware of the felt sense, you then bring to it a special quality of attention. One way I like to say this is, you sit down to get to know it better. I like to call this quality "interested curiosity." By bringing this interested curiosity into a relationship with the felt sense, you are open to sensing that which is there but not yet in words. This process of sensing takes time – it is not instant. So ideally there is a willingness to take that time, to wait, at the edge of not-yet-knowing what this is, patient, accepting, curious, and open. Slowly, you sense more. This can be a bit like coming into a darkened room and sitting, and as your eyes get used to the lower light, you sense more there than you had before. You could also have come into that room and then rushed away again, not caring to sense anything there. It is the caring to, the interest, the wanting to get to know it, that brings the further knowing.

There is not a trying to change anything. There is no doing something to anything. In this sense, this process is very accepting. We accept that this felt sense is here, just as it is, right now. We are interested in how it is. We want to know it, just as it is.

Yet there is something more than just accepting. In this interested curious

20

inner attention, there is also a confident expectation that this felt sense will change in its own way, that it will do something that Gene Gendlin calls "making steps." What is "making steps"?

The inner world is never static. When you bring awareness to it, it unfolds, moves, becomes its next step.

A woman is Focusing, let's say, on a heavy feeling in her chest which she feels is connected with a relationship with a friend. The Focuser recently left her job, and she has just discovered that the friend is applying for the position. She has been telling herself that this is not important, but the feeling of something wrong has persisted. Now she sits down to Focus.

She brings awareness into the throat-chest-stomach area of her body and she soon discovers this heavy feeling which has been around all week. She says hello to it. She describes it freshly: "heavy... also tight... especially in the stomach and chest." Then she sits with it to get to know it better. She is interested and curious. Notice how this interested and curious is the opposite of the telling herself that this is not important which she had been doing before. She waits, with this engaged accepting attention.

She can feel that this part of her is angry. "How could she? How could she do that?" it says about her friend. Ordinarily she would be tempted to tell herself that being angry is inappropriate, but this is Focusing, so she just says to this place, "I hear you," and keeps waiting. Interested and curious for the "more" that is there.

In a minute she begins to sense that this part of her is also sad. "Sad" surprises her; she didn't expect sad. She asks, "Oh, what gets you sad?" In response, she senses that it is something about being invalidated. She waits, there is more. Oh, something about not being believed! When she gets that, something about not being believed, a rush of memories comes, all the times she told her friend how difficult her boss was to work for. "It's as if she didn't believe me!" is the feeling.

Now our Focuser is feeling relief in her body. This has been a step. The emergence of sad after the anger was also a step. The Focusing process is a series of steps of change, in which each one brings fresh insight, and a fresh body relief, an aha! Is this the end? She could certainly stop here. But if she wanted to continue, she would go back to the "something about not being believed" feeling and again bring to it interested curiosity. It might be that there's something special for her about not being believed, something linked

21

to her own history, which again brings relief when it is heard and understood.

Focusing brings insight and relief, but that's not all it brings. It also brings new behavior. In the case of this woman, we can easily imagine that her way of being with her friend will now be more open, more appropriately trusting. It may also be that other areas of her life were bound up with this "not being believed" feeling, and they too will shift after this process. This new behavior happens naturally, easily, without having to be done by will power or effort. And this brings us to the third special quality of Focusing.

The third key quality or aspect which sets Focusing apart from any other method of inner awareness and personal growth is a radical philosophy of what facilitates change.

How do we change? How do we not change? If you are like many of the people who are drawn to Focusing, you probably feel stuck or blocked in one or more areas of your life. There is something about you, or your circumstances, or your feelings and reactions to things, that you would like to change. That is very natural. But let us now contrast two ways of approaching this wish to change.

One way assumes that to have something change, you must make it change. You must do something to it. We can call this the Doing/Fixing way.

The other way, which we can call the Being/Allowing way, assumes that change and flow is the natural course of things, and when something seems not to change, what it needs is attention and awareness, with an attitude of allowing it to be as it is, yet open to its next steps.

Our everyday lives are deeply permeated with the Doing/Fixing assumption.

When you tell a friend about a problem, how often is her response to give you advice on fixing the problem? Many of our modern therapy methods carry this assumption as well. Cognitive therapy, for example, asks you to change your self-talk. Hypnotherapy often brings in new images and beliefs to replace the old. So the Being/Allowing philosophy, embodied in Focusing, is a radical philosophy. It turns around our usual expectations and ways of viewing the world. It's as if I were to say to you that this chair you are sitting on would like to become an elephant, and if you will just give it interested attention it will begin to transform. What a wild idea! Yet that is how wild it sounds, to some deeply ingrained part of ourselves, when we are told that a fear that we have might transform into something which is not at all fear, if it is given interested attention.

When people who are involved in Focusing talk about the "wisdom of the body," this is what they mean: that the felt sense "knows" what it needs to become next, as surely as a baby knows it needs warmth and comfort and food. As surely as a radish seed knows it will grow into a radish. We never have to tell the felt sense what to become; we never have to make it change. We just need to provide the conditions which allow it to change, like a good gardener providing light and soil and water, but not telling the radish to become a cucumber.

This is a reprint from: *The Radical Acceptance of Everything: Living a Focusing Life*

Ann Weiser Cornell

Clearing a Space: A Centering Method for Enhancing Receptivity and Presence for the Classroom

Joan Klagsbrun, Ph.D.

Our body and mind are not two and not one. If you think your body and mind are two, that is wrong.
If you think that they are one, that is also wrong. Our body and mind are both two and one."
  —Shunryu Suzuki, Zen Mind, Beginner's Mind

How Stress Interferes with Receptivity to Learning

The educational experience is comprised of two aspects: teaching and learning. Although one might be tempted to view these aspects as one that is active (teaching) and one that is passive (learning), in truth, both are active. For good teaching to occur, the teacher needs to be competent and passionate about her topic and to have well-organized and relevant teaching materials. She must be present and connected to what she is teaching. Similarly, for real learning to occur, the student must not only be present in body, mind and in spirit, but must also have some readiness and intention to learn.

Students come to school under the burden of a large number of stressors. Undergraduates must deal with the intensity of a relatively unstructured campus life, their own adolescent dramas, and the issues of separating from parents and re-inventing themselves as young adults. Graduate students may face a continuation of those stressors from their undergraduate years, plus additional

25

ones. Some commute long distances, often in the evening, to get to and from school; many are engaged in school activities as they raise families or search for life partners; most are concerned about the financial pressures of being a student. For any student, attendant stresses often mean that while they may be physically present in class, it is difficult for them to be fully present intellectually and emotionally.

High stress levels are a direct impediment to a person's ability to learn effectively.

Students need to be taught methods of dealing with the stressors that keep them from being fully present in class. Many teachers understand how to achieve a sense of presence when stressed themselves, but few of them are well-versed in helping students to get into a state of receptivity at the beginning of a class. In my experience, and from the clinical experiences and research that my colleagues and I have done, (Grindler Katonah, 1999; Klagsbrun, 1999; Klagsbrun et al, 2006) Clearing A Space is an effective and original method for rapid stress reduction. I propose that the Clearing A Space method could be an explicit part of any teaching/learning curriculum, and would offer both teachers and students the opportunity to become more active and effective participants in the educational experience.

What is Clearing a Space?

Clearing A Space is five to ten minute induction into a state of reduced stress and enhanced receptivity. It differs from other stress-reduction methods in that it is a process that explicitly names and places aside each person's list of current stressors. It is both a means of becoming aware of one's stress load, and reducing it at the same time. Clearing A Space uses the metaphor of searching inside oneself, and allowing whatever obstacles one finds to feeling "fine or all clear" to be noted, tagged, separated from the self, and placed at the right distance away. Whether a student (or teacher) feels anxious, fearful, angry, scattered, fatigued, preoccupied or distracted, making some time to identify what is "between me and feeling fine or ready to be in class," and then "setting these issues aside" enables each person to be more present and receptive for the learning at hand.

Clearing A Space invites students to connect with themselves just as they are, in the privacy of their own minds and hearts. It invites each person to take an inventory of what is between her and feeling present and ready for class, and to then find a sense of what she would be like if all of those impediments to feeling good were removed. It is a way to resurrect a sense of well-being and presence, both of which enhance one's capacity for effective learning.

The Origins of Clearing a Space

Clearing A Space is the first step in a process called Focusing. In the 1960s, Eugene Gendlin, a philosopher, and Carl Rogers, a psychologist, carried out research which explored the question: "Why is some therapy successful in helping people make significant changes in their lives, and why is some therapy unsuccessful?"(Gendlin, 1981). They looked at variables such as the therapist's qualities of empathy, as well as the effect of particular approaches to therapy. To their surprise, what they discovered was that the factor that most accurately predicted success in therapy had nothing to do with either the qualities of the therapist, or the type of therapy being used. Rather, the most accurate predictor involved the client's capacity to be connected to his or her inner process.

Clients who were successful—who achieved significant positive change from their therapies—kept in touch with their inner process as they were talking. They did not spend time talking about something but from it. In recorded sessions, it was observed that these clients often spoke haltingly and tentatively, and seemed to be groping their way to an internal sense of what they were feeling in the moment. They intuitively knew when they had the right word or image or sentence to describe that feeling, because their bodies let go and relaxed when they found a satisfactory way to characterize it. These clients were the ones who got better in therapy over a year's time.

Gendlin studied how these clients connected to their inner felt sense. He then turned this naturally occurring process into a six-step method he named Focusing. He chose the name 'Focusing' because, like the lens of a camera, this process clarifies what is at first vague and unclear in the body by symbolizing it with a word, phrase, or image. Although the original intent of his Focusing method was to help people succeed in therapy, it soon became apparent that the Focusing method could also be useful in the fields of education, the expressive arts, theology, business and healthcare. Since Focusing is a generic skill, it can be utilized whenever a deeper and more personal understanding is sought.

As he continued to refine the Focusing system, Gendlin noticed that when practitioners initially engaged in naming their current issues, the Focusing process that followed was deeper and more effective. Eventually he incorporated a systematic way of recognizing and cataloging the stressors or issues of the moment, without becoming consumed by them. He called this preliminary step Clearing A Space.

Focusing, Clearing a Space and Relaxation

There is some research demonstrating that the inner bodily attention an individual develops through Focusing helps the body to relax (Gendlin, 1961;

Bernick 1969; Gendlin, 1999). This makes sense since we carry situations in our body as physical tension that is specific to each psychological issue—such as tightness in the stomach about one issue, shallow breathing and constriction about another, and tight shoulders about a third. When we try to turn our attention away from the problems, often the body retains the stress, tension, or agitation. Placing the generalized feeling of agitation or malaise or anger aside in one fell swoop doesn't usually work well. However, with Clearing A Space, we attend to how the body is carrying each stressor or problem, and then mentally place "all about that one" aside. This specificity allows us to relax the specific bodily tightness or constriction attached to a specific issue. The end result is usually a more relaxed and peaceful mind-body system.

Focusing, Clearing a Space and Improved School Performance
Research suggests that focusing works in very specific ways to help students improve their school performance. For example, in a series of 12 carefully designed experiments, Zimring found that college students who used focusing did significantly better than control groups on a number of cognitive tasks related to academic performance (Zimring, 1983, 1985; Zimring & Katz, 1988). First, he found that they did significantly better on the Stroop test, which required them to ignore distractions created by previously learned habits of thinking (Zimring, 1983). In another experiment, he found that students were also able to perform complex mental arithmetic more quickly after focusing (Zimring, 1983). Exploring the reasons why focusing improved performance on mental arithmetic, Zimring (1985) found that focusing improved recall of the internally generated stimuli necessary for that task. Exploring this further, he demonstrated that focusing increases recall by enriching the network of associations around new information. Students who used focusing not only formed more associations between new information and pre-existing ideas, they also formed completely new associations to the new information (Zimring & Katz, 1988). The increased associations, of course, resulted in increased learning.

A series of five studies (Zimring 1974; 1983; 1985; 1988; 1990) show that performance on complex mental tasks requiring attention to internally generated stimuli is increased by the first step of Focusing, Clearing A Space. In line with the idea that focusing enhances non automatic cognitive process, Focusers were found to do better on measures of creativity (Gendlin 1968), intuition Vandenbos 1971), flexible use of attention (Oberhoff 1990; Iberg 1990) and conceptual complexity (Fontana 1980). Focusers can maintain concentration and withstand distractions while attending to an internal body sense (Tamura 1987; Oishi 1989; Oberhoff 1990.)

Ways that Clearing a Space is Different from Other Contemplative Practices

There are some similarities between Clearing A Space and other contemplative practices such as the relaxation response and meditation. All three methods lead to a calming of the sympathetic system, and all involve turning inward and using silence as part of their practice. However, there are some interesting differences with Clearing A Space. First, instead of giving only bare attention to the stressor, as one does in meditation, in Clearing A Space one directs one's attention fully to a concern or difficulty, and then observes how the body is carrying that issue.

Imagery usually does not play a significant role in meditation. It is, however, an integral element of Clearing A Space. It can be creatively used by each person as a unique way to characterize and become empowered to place each stressful concern outside the body. Clearing a Space also has a relational dimension. This contrasts with relaxation and meditation, which are generally used as solo practices. Whether it is the teacher-student relationship that is improved (through the teacher's voice getting connected to the reduction in stress), or whether it is contact with another student (creating a sense of intimacy and connectedness), there is a communal benefit that comes from the relational aspect of this process. The class becomes engaged in a unified way, and shares a common practice.

What Happens During Clearing A Space
The important aspects of this easily taught process are:

We create a "frame" which has as its basic assumption that feeling "OK" is our natural state. The assumption is that our lives have presented us with a number of obstacles that currently block our ability to "feel OK".

We learn how to have a relationship with our "issues." We attempt to treat ourselves with an attitude of self-acceptance and kindness. This is not a forced acceptance of what feels unacceptable—it is simply an acknowledgement of whatever is there. It's as if we are saying "hello" to our issues and making a space for them.

We give a name to whatever we are sensing inside that is contributing to feeling stressed or tense or preoccupied. This might be the name of a recognizable issue such as frustration with my boss about not giving me a raise, which I know is connected to a tight and contracted feeling in my chest, or an unknown something that is unclear but distinctly felt in the body, i.e. a knot of dread in the pit of my stomach that I don't yet understand. Either way, we are empowered with a tool for identifying those sensations that are not yet symbolized though words.

29

We put each of these issues at the right distance away, outside the body, thus creating a sense of mastery. Some people use imagery to place the issues away— such as wrapping them up like a package and placing them next to where one is sitting; or placing them in boats and sending them out to sea or finding a spot where each one belongs. One student reported that her first issue was being given to a close friend who held it lovingly; a second issue was placed in a large see- through container by her side; and a third problem had to be sent to Kansas, hundreds of miles away.

Interestingly, the intelligence of the body/mind seems to know how and where each issue needs to be placed so that one gets respite from it. In this process, you are neither abandoning your problems nor confronting them, but merely parking them at a comfortable distance in order to be present for the task at hand (i.e. being present in class).

We discover our background sense. In addition to the inventory that comes from the body's experience of what it is carrying in the moment, we are asked to identify a background sense—that familiar quality that has become like the wallpaper we don't even see any more — that is there, coloring our whole experience. A background sense might be feeling driven, or sad, or pressured, or unprepared, or bored, or disconnected, or racing, or exhausted. The background sense might also be positive, such as feeling excited, or eager, or content. By discovering this background sense, we get a more global sense of how we are feeling.

Finally we take a minute or two to dwell in the cleared or clearer space. We enable ourselves to experience what it would be like without all those tangles that are connected to being stressed or tense or distracted or scattered. This is an important moment—we get a glimpse of what it would be like to experience ourselves without those familiar concerns and weighty issues. Without those burdens, most people report feeling lighter, less weighed down, more how they are at their best. They describe this feeling variously as feeling calm, or spacious, or finding a bigger perspective, or getting connected to their aliveness and energy. They can often sense their inherent healthiness. This experience is often felt as freeing and empowering. In a classroom environment, tapping into these feelings before turning attention to learning can vitalize the learning environment.

How to Use Clearing a Space as Part of your Curriculum
There are two ways that Clearing A Space can be utilized at the start of a class. In one way, the teacher begins the class by taking the students through the protocol. Students work silently within themselves, giving themselves some needed silence and guidance to name and clear out the issues weighing on them

or if they are in a positive place, to spend time reviewing what has contributed to their feeling so good. When the teacher leads the exercise, the tone of voice and acceptance and permission given can create a positive relationship and a sense from the students that their full selves are welcome in the class. The teacher is then experienced as validating them as they are, as well as offering something of value that assists students in making the transition from their busy lives into the classroom environment.

The second way to incorporate Clearing A Space into your class involves students finding a partner and taking turns reading each other the protocol. In this alternative model, students can choose to keep their issues silent or if they feel safe and comfortable with their fellow student, could say out loud what was in their way of being fully present for class that day. When a student shares with a fellow student, either by following the process out loud or in silence, there is a bond and an intimacy that has many benefits: it reduces the sense of isolation which many students face; it creates the possibility of new friendships; and it reduces stress by feeling that your situation is held and validated by a peer, and as a result it often increases mood. Having someone hold the space while you do this personal and inner reflection can also allow you to go deeper in clearing out the difficulties because it taps into the power of human connection.

The following are instructions for either the teacher or the students to read. If the peer method is being used, instead of pausing for the prescribed amount of time, the partners can give each other a signal, such as lifting a finger, to indicate that they are ready for the next instruction.

1. When you are ready, you might want to close your eyes, get comfortable in your chair, let yourself to take a few slow breaths, and then allow your awareness to gently come into the center of your body. (PAUSE 10 seconds) Ask yourself, "How am I feeling on the inside right now?"(PAUSE 5 seconds) or, if that doesn't work, ask "What's in the way of feeling fine today?" (PAUSE 5 seconds) Don't answer, but let what comes in your body do the answering. Take your time and wait for a felt sense of a concern to form. (PAUSE 10 seconds) If, however, you're feeling all fine today, just stay with that good feeling.

2. Now see if there is a word, a phrase, or an image that captures the quality of how one of the concerns or good feeling feels in your body. (PAUSE 5 seconds) Say the word, phrase, or image back to yourself, and check to see if it fits the sense you have there exactly.

3. Now give this concern your accepting, friendly attention for a few moments

(PAUSE 5 seconds), but then put it aside for a while by imagining that you are placing it outside of your body, in a safe place. Sometimes it helps to imagine that you're sitting on a park bench, and each concern can be wrapped up like a package, and placed on the park bench next to you. (PAUSE 10 seconds)

4. Notice if you feel a little lighter or clearer inside without that one. (PAUSE)

5. Now again, bring your attention inside and ask, "Except for that, am I feeling fine?" (PAUSE 5 seconds) Wait and see if something else wants your attention next.

6. If something else comes up, wait for a felt sense of that concern to form (PAUSE 10 seconds), and see if a word, phrase, or image captures the quality of how this concern feels in your body. (PAUSE 5 seconds) And then, after spending a little time with it, place it outside your body in a safe place as well. (PAUSE 10 seconds) Notice if you feel a little lighter or clearer inside without that one. (PAUSE)

7. Now, in addition to those issues and concerns, most of us have a background sense – always feeling a little anxious, or sad, or harried, or tense – see if you can find a background sense that's there for you today, and place that out as well. (PAUSE 10 seconds)

8. Now bring your attention back inside your body and you might find that there is a clearer space there. (PAUSE 5 seconds) Welcome this space and allow yourself to rest in it (PAUSE 5 seconds). There's nothing to do – just allow yourself to be. Some people find that this is a place where you can notice that you are not your problems, even though you have them. You are much larger. (PAUSE 10 seconds) See if a word or an image captures how it feels in the clear or clearer space. (PAUSE 10 seconds) Say this word or phrase back to yourself and see if it is a good fit. You might want to spend a little time with it. (PAUSE 5 seconds).

9. Now, turn your attention back to the class that is about to begin (PAUSE 5 seconds). See if you can find an intention for yourself in relation to the class material, perhaps something you want to either learn or share, or a question you may have.

Benefits of Clearing a Space
There are many advantages to teachers and students when using this mind/body tool. First, Clearing A Space connects mind/body and spirit – the process is physical (works with the body), mental (works with meaning), and spiritual (creates a broader perspective). It also connects both sides of the brain. As Le

Doux put it (1998), "[Focusing] seems to be the process of putting feelings into words that enable the left and right brains to become integrated, ... linking the right brain 'felt sense' and the left brain's verbal account. These links may be important because they allow the maximum information to flow freely between the two hemispheres".

Clearing A Space releases bodily tension. Usually our concerns and issues are clumped together like a ball of yarn so that we feel a mass of worry or a general sense of sadness or tension. The different stressors or problems easily can become enmeshed with each other and then they seem to weigh us down more. When named and separated, strand-by- strand, however, each concern gets our full attention, and then when removed we can feel a lightening in its absence.

Clearing A Space invites us to treat ourselves with Compassion. One of the tenets of Focusing is to greet whatever emerges with friendliness, gentleness, and respect. While critical and judgmental attitudes close off lines of communication, a welcoming attitude allows us to hear from parts of ourselves that have been previously inaccessible.

Clearing A Space often elicits a deep sense of well-being in the body. After having cleared a space, students and teachers often discover an inner sense of well-being. Having set aside current stressors, we can more easily connect to a positive core identity. This cleared space is usually more than a neutral space of merely being all right; it often seems to open onto a wider spiritual experience. Many students report feeling calm, spacious, at peace, and in harmony with themselves.

Clearing A Space is transferable to a variety of other circumstances the student may face. In addition to increasing presence in the classroom, it can be utilized for stress reduction when preparing to study, write a paper, give a presentation, or deal with personal problems.

Finally, in my experience, students deeply appreciate the 10 minutes to collect and center themselves, and are so much more present that the "lost time "of teaching is made up by their increased attentiveness and engagement with the class material. One measure I have for the effectiveness of this tool is punctuality. I have asked students who arrive late to please wait outside the class until the Clearing A Space time is complete so as not to disturb the others. Rarely does anyone arrive late! And if by chance I forget to start class with it, I am reminded to stop and help them clear a space. In my evaluations each year, students mention how helpful Clearing A Space was at the start of class. They report that it helps them with the transition to school or from one class to another. Getting themselves physically to class doesn't assure that students are truly present. This short and effective method seems to help them ready themselves for a more productive learning experience.

Conclusion

Clearing A Space is a short and efficient centering process. It can be accomplished when students are guided to connect briefly with their issues, to bring attention into themselves in a silent way, to separate one concern or problem from another so they are not held in a confused clump, and to set the whole of each issue aside for a while. This process, whether done as a whole class or in pairs, brings a bodily relief and a sense of becoming more centered. Through this process we realize that while we each have certain issues that are weighing on us, we can observe and tag them and place them aside. The process of observing them creates the awareness that we are not our problems, and allows us to perceive that essential part of ourselves who is separate from our problems.. This connection to an unburdened or larger self typically creates a sense of inner calm or peace.

Clearing A Space also frees up attention for the class. The students and teacher have attended to themselves in a caring Compassionate way, and placed aside their burdens of the day. They are then more ready to bring attention to the class material and to be more engaged in the learning process.

REFERENCES

Bernick, N., & Oberlander, M. (1969). Effect of verbalization and two different modes of experiencing on pupil size. Perception and Psychophysics, 3, 327–339.

Gendlin, E.T. & J.I. Berlin (1961). Galvanic skin response correlates of different modes of experiencing. Journal of Clinical Psychology, 17 (1), 73-77.

Gendlin, E.T. (1981) Focusing. Bantam: New York.

Gendlin, E.T. (1999) The First Step of Focusing Provides a Superior Stress-Reduction Method. The Folio 18 (1), 178.

Grindler Katonah, D. (1999). Clearing A Space with someone who has Cancer The Folio 18 (1), 19.

Grindler Katonah, D. (1999) Focusing and Cancer: A Psychological Tool as an Adjunct Treatment for Adaptive Recovery. The Folio. 18 (1), 18.
Klagsbrun, J. (1999). Focusing, Illness and Health Care. The Folio. 18 (1), 162.

Klagsbrun, J. et al (2006) Focusing and Expressive Arts in Therapy as a Complementary Treatment for Women with Breast Cancer, Creativity in Mental Health, 1(1), 101-137.

Le Doux, J. (1998). The Emotional Brain: The Mysterious Underpinnings of Emotional Life. New York: Simon & Schuster

Zimring, F. M., & Balcombe, J. (1974). Cognitive operations in two measures of handling emotionally relevant material. Psychotherapy: Theory, Research and Practice, 11(3), 226–228

Zimring, F.R. (1983). Attending to feelings and cognitive performance. Journal of Research and Personality, 17 (3) 288-299.Zimring, F.R. (1985). The effect of attending to feeling on memory for internally generated stimuli. Journal of Research and Personality, 19 (2) 170-184.

Zimring, F.R., & Katz, K. (1988). Self-focus and relational knowledge. Journal of Research and Personality, 22 (3) 273-289.

Zimring, F. (1990). Cognitive processes as a cause of psychotherapeutic change: self-initiated processes. In G. Lietaer, J. Rombauts, & R. Van Balen (Eds.), Client-Centered and Experiential Psychotherapy inthe Nineties (pp. 361–380). Leuven: Leuven University Press.

Journal of Pedagogy, Pluralism, and Practice Online journal of Lesley Univiersity Issue 12, Summer 2007

Summary of Zimring Research on Clearing a Space

Mary Hendricks, Ph.D.

Research suggests that focusing works in very specific ways to help students improve their school performance. For example, in a series of 12 carefully designed experiments, Zimring found that college students who used focusing did significantly better than control groups on a number of cognitive tasks related to academic performance (Zimring, 1983, 1985; Zimring & Katz, 1988). First, he found that they did significantly better on the Stroop test, which required them to ignore distractions created by previously learned habits of thinking (Zimring, 1983). In another experiment, he found that students were also able to perform complex mental arithmetic more quickly after focusing (Zimring, 1983). Exploring the reasons why focusing improved performance on mental arithmetic, Zimring (1985) found that focusing improved recall of the internally generated stimuli necessary for that task. Exploring this further, he demonstrated that focusing increases recall by enriching the network of associations around new information. Students who used focusing not only formed more associations between new information and pre-existing ideas, they also formed completely new associations to the new information (Zimring & Katz, 1988). The increased associations, of course, resulted in increased learning.

A wealth of clinical experience suggests that the benefits college students obtained from focusing are also be available to younger children. The consensus among clinicians is that children learn focusing even more easily than adults (e.g., Conway, 1977; Marder, 1977, 1988; McGuire, 1986; McMahon & Bruinix, 1991; Neagu, 1986, 1988; Santen, 1990, 1999; Stapert, 1997). Most first graders learn it immediately when it is first shown to them, while older children and adults vary, some being able to do it immediately, some requiring six to eight hours of teaching.

Thus, current data suggest that second and third graders will perform measurably better in mathematics after focusing; and it is reasonable to expect that they will perform better in other subjects as well. In addition, children who learn focusing should be better able to deal with stress, and should therefore show fewer physical and psychological symptoms related to stress.

Zimring, F.R. (1983). Attending to feelings and cognitive performance. *Journal of Research and Personality, 17* (3) 288-299.
Zimring, F.R. (1985). The effect of attending to feeling on memory for internally generated stimuli. *Journal of Research and Personality, 19* (2) 170-184.
Zimring, F.R., & Katz, K. (1988). Self-focus and relational knowledge. *Journal of Research and Personality, 22* (3) 273-289.

Another summary:
A series of five studies (Zimring 1974; 1983; 1985; 1988; 1990) show that performance on complex mental tasks requiring attention to internally generated stimuli is increased by the first step of Focusing, Clearing A Space. In line with the idea that focusing enhances non automatic cognitive process, Focusers were found to do better on measures of creativity (Gendlin 1968), intuition Vandenbos 1971), flexible use of attention (Oberhoff 1990; Iberg 1990) and conceptual complexity (Fontana 1980). Focusers can maintain concentration and withstand distractions while attending to an internal body sense (Tamura 1987; Oishi 1989; Oberhoff 1990.)

Zimring, F. (1990). Cognitive processes as a cause of psychotherapeutic change: self-initiated processes. In G. Lietaer, J. Rombauts, & R. Van Balen (Eds.), *Client-Centered and Experiential Psychotherapy In the Nineties* (pp. 361–380). Leuven: Leuven University Press.
Zimring, F. M., & Balcombe, J. (1974). Cognitive operations in two measures of handling emotionally relevant material. *Psychotherapy: Theory, Research and Practice, 11*(3), 226–228.

Sarah: Focusing and Play Therapy with a
Six Year Old Child

Diana Marder, Ph.D.

The Folio1997

Sarah was six years old when her mother and stepfather first brought her to me. Her apparent understanding of the purpose of therapy belied her petite body and high, piping voice: when I asked her if she had any problems, she replied that "Sometimes I go potty in my pants, I have bad dreams, and I feel sad because I miss my daddy."

Sarah's parents had divorced a little over two years before and the family had endured a difficult custody battle. Sarah now lived with her mother, sister, and stepfather, and apparently had good relationships with all of them. Nevertheless Sarah was displaying many symptoms of anxiety-she wet the bed, 'played with herself' a great deal, had a difficult time making decisions, and seemed to feel that she needed to be perfect. Most of all, she was reluctant to express negative feelings or anger. Sarah would be with her father, who lived out of state, for a long summer visit, and her mother was concerned that Sarah was too much of a 'pleaser' to defend herself against her father's sometimes inappropriate behaviors.

I saw Sarah weekly for a total of twenty-nine sessions (every other week toward the end). As I reviewed my notes in preparation for this paper, I was quite surprised to find that we had had only four actual Focusing sessions. I had had the impression that there were many more, perhaps because these sessions were so pivotal in her therapy.

From the beginning, Sarah fluctuated in her ability to tolerate her more difficult feelings. When Sarah first entered the playroom, she focused on a poster of children displaying many different emotions. I asked her to point to a picture "that you sometimes feel like," and she pointed to a sad face, saying "I felt sad when mommy and daddy got divorced." When I asked her to draw a picture of this, however, she drew a bright happy picture. Later she willingly drew a picture of herself "sad because I miss my daddy" and admitted that she was scared that "Mom and dad won't figure things out." Finally, tired of all this emotion, Sarah asked to play, and we took out the Play Doh. She played creatively, resourcefully, and with great energy, and I could see the health and vitality that existed side by side with her struggles.

During the next eight sessions, Sarah and I worked in individual play therapy. I soon realized that she was struggling with both angry, aggressive feelings, and a desire to be coddled and babied. She alternated between expressing these aggressive and regressive feelings, and retreating to the safer although highly creative artistic play that she so much enjoyed. One session she played with puppets, making them bite each other, then played with the doll house, unable to decide whether one of the dolls was a baby or an eight-year-old child. The next session, she spent the entire hour intently making multicolored candy and carefully wrapping it. At times Sarah seemed very invested in things that were cute and pretty. Her responses to story telling cards included "a very sweet and cute monkey, a cute little baby just waking up from its nap, and a really cute little puppy." Immediately after this she produced a sand tray full of "pretty" flowers and trees, but made no mention of the warlike Indian and soldier who were facing each other in the center of the scene. Sarah's true self seemed to be struggling to break through her protective identity of a "cute little girl", which was reinforced by nearly everyone who commented on how adorably petite she was.

During the next few weeks Sarah seemed to retreat slightly from dealing with her feelings. At home she seemed troubled and rather fragile, and the techniques I regularly use in therapy to elicit feelings from children were often ineffective. In retrospect, it seemed obvious that her troubled feelings probably had to do with an upcoming visit with her father. Sarah ended up enjoying her visit, and drew only bright, happy pictures about the things that she had done. But by the next session Sarah was again grappling with aggressive feelings-she made pretty little objects out of Play Doh, finished with a Play Doh man, and at the end of the session cheerfully smashed it with her fist, saying "You're dead." The next week Sarah's mother reported that she had started to talk more about her feelings and seemed less frustrated. That week in therapy she continued the by-now familiar pattern of aggression followed by retreat; first she took a toy gun and shot every doll in the room, then sat down to cheerfully make a clay pizza.

The following week, the tenth session, I taught Sarah Focusing without prior planning. Sarah and her mother came in together and her mother explained that Sarah was very upset about being teased by a friend at school. I asked Sarah if she'd like me to show her something I sometimes did when I had a bad feeling that wouldn't go away, and she readily agreed. I asked her if she could find the bad feeling inside, and she did this easily. Then I suggested that she listen and see if it had anything to tell her. "He didn't mean it", she said. Her demeanor changed immediately and she had no interest in any more talk; the issue was gone and she was ready to play. Something seemed freed-up inside, for Sarah began playing with clay in a much more animated fashion then she previously had. She talked about wanting to make it perfect. I thought maybe she was ready to deal with the issue of perfectionism, and I commented "That doesn't happen very often does it?" She fervently answered "That's for sure." I asked how would it be if it was almost perfect; she replied "That would be really good".

The next two sessions Sarah again absorbed herself in playing with clay, painting, and making a sand tray about a "pretty lady" on her way to see her husband. Then came a session that was critical in terms of Sarah's use of Focusing to free up some of her stuck feelings. Sarah's mother reported that Sarah had been clingy and tearful recently. "Sarah", I said, "can you find that bad feeling inside you?"

"It's hiding," she replied after a moment.

I handed her a stuffed animal." Can you see if it will hide in the teddy bear?" Sarah placed the bear next to her stomach and then up to her ear. I thought that she was just playing, staying away from the uncomfortable feelings, but in a moment she replied, "It's about too many things happening".

"Oh. Too many things happening. What are they?"

"I forgot," she replied.

I reached over for a drawing pad and some magic markers (always with me when I see a child). I drew a small person with a sad face, glanced at Sarah and began to sketch the pattern of her clothes. Intrigued, she grabbed the markers and began energetically coloring the person. (I have yet to see a child who is not intrigued by my drawing them, the more so because they are totally

41

unintimidated by my primitive attempts!) I quickly drew six cloud shapes in a circle around the person and said" These are for all the things that are happening." Something about the physical presence of spaces to be filled.

The following week we had another crucial Focusing session. Sarah had been in a bad mood all afternoon but said that she did not want to talk about it. "Sarah," I said, "you can let the feeling talk just to you; you don't have to tell me and your mother if you don't want to. How about that?"

"Okay," she answered. She was quiet for a minute, then pointed to her stomach.

"What does it feel like?" I asked.

"Jumpy and angry; it's mad and it doesn't want to talk to anyone."

"Can you try being very nice and friendly to it?"

"No! I'm mad at it."

I suggested to Sarah that she had plenty of room inside to have both feelings and that the jumpy, angry feeling probably had a good reason for feeling that way.

"It sure does! People have been bugging me and pushing me on the playground all day!" After a pause of a few seconds she said in a tone of excited discovery, "I think part of the reason I'm so mad is that I didn't get to say good-bye to mom in the morning." Turning to her mother, she said," You were already asleep and daddy said not to wake you." Sarah's mother was understanding about this and said that maybe they could tell daddy that it was okay for Sarah to come in and say good-bye in the morning. After this Sarah insisted that her mother come to the play room with us, where she engaged in more witch-stomping. Later Sarah's mother reported that during the next week, Sarah had continued expressing anger more frequently.

During the next few sessions, things seemed to be winding down. Sarah had few difficulties to report and she was wetting herself less often at night. We decided to hold sessions only every other week. During the twenty-seventh session, Sarah's mother reported that Sarah had become in touch with a three-year-old child inside herself and that this three-year-old was much angrier and sadder than Sarah herself. At the next session, Sarah reported that when she was playing a game with her family, her three-year-old was sad that she wasn't winning. Sarah had talked to the three-year-old and told her 'I know you feel

42

sad, but maybe you'll win the next game". Then she felt better. The three year old also wet the bed whenever Sarah took off her "good-nights" (absorbent underwear for bed-wetting). When I suggested that Sarah ask the three-year-old what she could do to help, the three-year-old said that she was scared and that Sarah couldn't help her. "What would you like to say to your three-year-old now?" I asked. Sarah told her that she felt sad and wanted her to stop. The three-year-old replied that she would try, and Sarah was satisfied. At this point I felt that Sarah, with the assistance of her mother, was becoming her own therapist, and no longer needed me. We decided that the next session would be our last. During the last session Sarah drew me a wonderful good-bye picture with a caption that was straightforward, cheerful, and unapologetic-a style that seemed to be becoming her own.

When play therapy works, I am frequently at a loss to explain exactly why it was successful. There is rarely a direct, observable relationship between events in the play therapy and changes in the child. In the case of Sarah, the power of Focusing was no more directly explicable. There were only four Focusing sessions; in only two of these sessions did Sarah experience a "shift"; in none of the sessions did she deal directly with her ambivalence about aggression and anger or about regression versus growth. Nevertheless, each of these sessions seemed to be an important turning point in the therapy; each followed by perceptible behavioral changes. What follows, therefore, is a group of loose hypotheses concerning the power of Focusing in children.

1. It is important to note that, in spite of her troubled feelings, Sarah was in many ways a sophisticated and well-functioning child, relatively at home in the world of feelings It was crucial, too, that she had a very supportive parent, willing to not only accept all of her feelings, but also to make adjustments in her schedule to help meet Sarah's needs. This kind of concrete receptivity to a child's needs is, I believe, enormously helpful in allowing the child to be more receptive to his or her own feelings. Focusing always involves the creation of a friendly supportive "other" inside; with children it seems very important that there also be a friendly "other" outside in their day-to-day lives. Although I have used bits and pieces of Focusing in therapy with children less friendly with feelings, it is rare for me to find a child with whom Focusing can become a major modality. My experience is that troubled children simply do not have the anxiety tolerance to sit with something really difficult, or even to listen to suggestions on how to be gentle with it. The lives of these children seem to be so filled with difficult feelings that they dare not attend to them or they would be completely overwhelmed; because they experience their outside world as unsafe, they do not have a safe place inside. Helping these children find or create such a place would be a crucial first step in their therapy if Focusing is to be used. I have recently experimented with teaching whole families a "safe place" exercise

and thus far the response has been very positive; it remains to be seen if this can serve as a transition to Focusing.

2. For Sarah it seemed important to be able to fully express her anger against herself. It was only after refusing to be friendly to her upsetting feelings, and expressing her anger at these feelings, that she was able to listen to them in an open way and learn what was under them. I am coming to believe that the expression of anger against the self can be a crucial part of freeing up aggressive feelings in individuals of all ages. It may be that expressing this anger at the part of the self that is problematic can help prevent this anger from turning into entrenched self-hatred. Perhaps we need to be especially careful that, when we work to create a friendly hearing for feelings, we also create space for this type of anger.

3. Focusing for Sarah, as for adults, seems to free up energy in a way that is not directly related to content. It is as if the energy released by "unsticking" an area of feeling becomes available to use in many ways, and that many different kinds of feelings also become unstuck in the process. This seemed to be the case, especially, following the session in which Sarah worked on her "nervous" feelings about a friend encouraging wrong behavior. Although that session did not even deal with issues of anger or assertion, it was followed by a burst of more freely assertive and expressive behavior. That session also illustrated the next point.

4. Shifts appear unnecessary for Focusing to perform its magic. I believe the experience of major shift is important both for the insight and relief that it brings, and for the enormous feeling of empowerment that comes from being able to solve one's own difficulties from inside. But there is also a great deal of empowerment that comes from the process of simply taking charge of one's feelings, in the sense of not being a victim-sorting through, putting this here, and that there, listening to this now, and that later, and simply acknowledging a feeling as unmanageable for the moment but definitely not forever. Children often have so little power in their daily lives; to discover a powerful stance toward their own feelings must be enormously self-enhancing.

Very little modification of technique seems necessary to focus with verbal children above the age of six years old. I very frequently use clearing a space, not in the sense of actually clearing problems from the body (although I do this with older children), but simply to raise issues and for the relief of naming things. I don't know whether or not the drawings are necessary, but they certainly engage the attention of the child who is resistant to talking about bad feelings. I keep my language simple, usually limiting directions to "Find the

44

place inside where you feel it," and "See what that feeling wants to say to you." From that point on, creativity and ingenuity may be required. The game of projecting the feeling into a toy or stuffed animal often seems effective. I believe this is because it allows the child to take on the power and security of being the bigger, nurturing, caring presence. This, in turn, allows the child to take on the Focusing attitude of being separate from, but in caring relationship to her feelings. In this regard, children are no different from adults; it is this relationship that makes healing possible.

Focusing Training
Class 1-2 Home Practice
Diana Marder Ph.D.

Use the exercise below any time something has stressed or disturbed you. You might want to do it before starting class in the morning, between classes, or at lunch time.

Space is provided below to record the times you use it.

One Minute Clearing a Space

Use whenever something leaves you uncomfortable in any way

Take some deep slow breaths while noticing what the issue feels like in your body. Give it time to develop and clarify.

See if there is a word or phrase to describe your bodily felt sense.

Say to yourself, "Yes, I really do feel [your word/phrase]."

Stay with the word and feeling in a friendly way for another 10-15 ".

Take a very deep breath and put the feeling to one side, where you can go back to it if you like, when you have time.

Notes
Day/time   **Word/phrase for bodily felt sense**

_____

FOCUSING

LEARN FROM THE MASTERS

TRAINING MANUAL II

Focusing for an Action Step

Lucinda Gray, Ph.D.

Finding a Right Action Step

We all have a lot "on our minds". We carry many work, personal and relationship issues around all the time in our bodies. Many of these things want to be listened to. They express a need for personal attention through feeling, emotion and/or sensation, signaling that your deeper self wants to be heard. These issues are alive in us all the time and when they are not listened to, not acknowledged, they act as distractions and keep us from being fully present in the current moment. They are a burden of unattended feelings that get in the way of feeling good. The truth is that you carry within you the wisdom you need to work through your issues and creatively discover the most effective solutions.

This article is a preliminary description of how to use the Focusing process to effectively explore an issue, discover exactly what it is that needs to be changed, and then find an action step that fits for you. Clearing a Space is a necessary first step toward finding a right action step. Only within the cleared space, when other issues have been put aside, do you have room for Felt Sensing; going more deeply into the issue to discover exactly what it is that needs to change, and then check in more deeply with yourself to find what to do to improve your situation. Finally you can use Focusing methods to be sure that the action step you are contemplating truly fits for you, and for the situation as you experience it.

Preparing For Inner Work

As you prepare to spend time with yourself, recall the Focusing Attitude—that approach of gentle curiosity toward whatever you find inside; nonjudgmental acceptance. Isn't it interesting that I have this right now; I wonder what this is about for me? Adopt an attitude of benign curiosity toward whatever is there.

Stage 1— Clearing a Space

There are many different versions of Clearing a Space. Here I will guide you through my own favorite method.

Come Home to your Body

First, come into your center in your body, follow the central energy channel that goes from your throat all the way down to your pelvis, and find the place where you usually feel things, usually somewhere between chest and stomach. Track your breath as you inhale and exhale, as a way of bringing awareness inside. Don't rush; this stage should take about 60 seconds.

Invite Your Inner Self to Come Up

When you are ready, ask yourself inside, in that center place -What's between me and feeling just fine right now? Then just wait and see what comes. There are several ways the question can be posed. As you repeat the exercise a few times you will discover how best to frame the question; what works for you. Here are a couple of examples: You might say to yourself- If it wasn't for this or that I would feel just fine right now. Or, you might propose to yourself- Everything in my life is just wonderful right now. Then notice what comes in your body in response.

Your body may answer with a sensation or feeling. If so, then ask if you know what this is about in your life right now. The information inside doesn't always come in the form of body sensation, sometimes a thought may come first. If it comes as a thought, then check in your body to see if there is a body sense that goes with the thought. The important part is to connect the body sense with the thought.

Make a safe space for the new information, and take a few moments to acknowledge it. Can you own it as your own? Acknowledging it by recognizing it and perhaps naming it, and staying with it even for just a moment allows it to be put on the shelf for now. Sometimes when it is acknowledged it will just seem to move out of your body, dissolve and fade out of your awareness.

52

Return to your center and check with your body sensation to be sure that the issue was actually put aside. You may have to work with this a little bit to find ways that work for you. You might have to promise this particular issue that you won't ignore it, that you will return to feel-think about it again. Maybe you need to promise it that you will hold a specific time to feel-think about it again.

Now you can ask inside what else might be calling for your attention. One by one you acknowledge and set aside the issues that are calling for your attention, using the same process as before. Begin by staying in your center and asking again.........Except for this thing that I just put aside, everything else in my life is just fine? Again, wait inside for your body to tell you what's comes next.

Meet the next issue or feeling with the same caring attention, not going too far into it but sitting with the feeling long enough to touch, identify and acknowledge it, and then gently invite it to be put aside for now, so that you see what else might be there. Gradually you will develop a pile of issues and feelings that you have set aside and you will begin to feel that clear space opening in your center.

Enjoy Your Inner Clear Space

Spend a few moments with that quiet inner space which is your deeper self, separate from your issues and problems. Notice that when you have acknowledged all that you have been carrying, there is a sense of relief, peace and clarity. Don't rush; take at least a few minutes to enjoy the clear space before you go on. Now your body/mind is clear and you can work and think more effectively.

Stage 2
Felt Sensing

Now you can choose a question to ask of your deeper self. As you stay with the clear space ask.......for example........

What do I most need for myself today?

or, What do I want/need today from this class, or this meeting?

What do I want for today at school or work?

When I look over my life, what feels most important for me at this time?

When I think of my future do I have a sense of what I might need/want for myself; regarding work, regarding school, regarding relationships?

Here it is especially important to take time to allow your inner knowing to take form. There is a "more" there if you wait for it. Pause and wait patiently inside, in your body, for something to come in response to your question. You may need several minutes. You may want to hold the image of the problem situation or stay with the feeling sensation. Let it form gradually, giving it time to fill in the space.

Stage 3
Letting Words or Images Come directly from the Felt Sense

Stay with your body sensation. Get the idea that words or images can come directly from a bodily felt knowing. Maybe a word or two or an image could come that seems to fit perfectly with your body sense. If something comes sit quietly with it, checking with your body sensation to see if this word does indeed match your feeling. Go back and forth between the word/s or image and the sensation/feeling. Wait until words or images come that seem to fit the feeling. Resonate by going back and forth between the felt sense and the symbolization. As you resonate you will notice a deepening sense of the rightness of the words/images

Stage 4
Finding an Action Step

Take time with the information that came. Ask what step you could take today to help bring about the situation or outcome you want. Maybe it is only a small step for right now. Wait patiently for an answer to come. Again taking time is important here; take at least a minute or two. Make a space to gently receive whatever comes. You want an action step that feels right, so spend some time resonating with what came. Sometimes asking for a step helps you get more clarity on the exact nature of the problem.

Stage 5
Rechecking That Action Step

When something comes, try it on by bringing it back into your body center and checking to see how it feels inside when you imagine taking this action. Stay with this for a few minutes, bringing awareness back and forth from the vision of taking the action step to the body sense that comes with it.

Be willing to listen to your body knowing about this. Maybe this step feels exactly right, a true expression of your nature, and fitting for the situation. Maybe it doesn't. If it isn't right, then is there some change that could allow it to feel better for you?

If you don't now have an answer, just promise your inner self you will check in again later today and tomorrow or next week. If no right action step comes, ask your inner wisdom for a small step that feels right for you.

Stage 6
Receiving

Whatever information you receive, appreciate it and make a safe space for it. Take some time to be grateful for the gift of your inner self. Enjoy the feeling inside that comes with listening to your deeper self in this respectful way. Take a few minutes to relax and complete in any way you want.

The Power of Listening
Ann Weiser Cornell, Ph.D.

A paper presented to the 13th International Focusing Conference, Shannon, Ireland, May, 2001

Abstract
We discuss the purposes of listening, and compare Rogers' stated purpose for "reflection of feelings" with Gendlin's purpose for reflection within a session that includes Focusing. Three purposes for listening are given, corresponding to three ways that listening facilitates Focusing process. Listening is then defined as making a statement that says back what the other person (focuser, client, partner) just said, exactly or in paraphrase, with no intention of changing or adding anything essential or of making any change in the other person's experience. Listening, as defined here, is not asking questions or making suggestions. We note that the linguistic form of listening responses changes as the purpose changes. We explore some linguistic forms that help listening do its work and accomplish its three purposes. We conclude that when listening is used with sensitivity and skill, little or no guiding is needed, especially between Focusing partners.

The Purpose of Listening
Why would we say back what someone else is saying? In ordinary life, repeating another person's words is just as likely to get you an angry look as a grateful

one. Yet in the special world of Focusing therapy and counseling, and the even more circumscribed world of Focusing partnership, repeating back is the key, the essence, the sine qua non.

Why?

Carl Rogers was not the first to repeat back a client's words, but he is the one who made it a well-known technique, taught in counseling courses and practiced worldwide. During his lifetime, the technique called "reflection of feelings" became so widely used, and in many cases so misunderstood, that a backlash was created, detractors mocking the therapist who merely repeats a client's words. Responding to this backlash, Rogers (who wrote in 1980 that the word "reflect" had come to make him cringe) clarified the purposes for repeating someone's words:

I have come to a double insight. From my point of view as therapist, I am not trying to "reflect feelings." I am trying to determine whether my understanding of the client's inner world is correct — whether I am seeing it as he or she is experiencing it at this moment. Each response of mine contains the unspoken question, "Is this the way it is in you? Am I catching just the color and texture and flavor of the personal meaning you are experiencing right now? If not, I wish to bring my perception in line with yours."

On the other hand, I know that from the client's point of view we are holding up a mirror of his or her current experiencing. The feelings and personal meanings seem sharper when seen through the eyes of another, when they are deflected. (1986b)

So Rogers saw the therapist's purpose for listening as checking with the client to make sure the therapist's understanding fit or matched the client's "inner world." At the same time, he saw that the client was receiving something more from having their "feelings and personal meanings" reflected, something more than could be predicted from the simple activity of checking understanding.

Eugene Gendlin, once Rogers' student, became interested in what he called "the client's side of the therapeutic process." (1984) He became interested in why some clients were vastly more helped by therapy than others. An important part of this question was why some clients were more able to get positive benefit from the therapist's reflection of their "feelings and personal meanings."

What do we assume the client will do with a listening response?

We hope and assume that clients will check the response, not against what they said or thought, but against some inner being, place, datum... "the felt sense"; we have no ordinary word for that.

An effect might then be felt, an inward loosening, a resonance. What seemed to be there was expressed and heard. It need not be said again. For some moments there is an easing inside. (In theoretical terms the interpersonal response has carried that forward.) Soon something further comes. What was there turns out to have more to it.

We hope that clients will check not only what we say, but also what they say, against that inward one. (1984, p. 82)

Gendlin called that which the client needs to check with the "felt sense." He was the first to identify and name this essential move: that the client checks what comes with something inside, directly felt. His research showed that this checking made the difference between success and failure in therapy. (That Rogers was impacted by Gendlin is shown by the fact that, writing about empathy in 1980, he cites Gendlin's work as a key reason that empathy is effective.)

Gendlin shifted the therapist's purpose for listening. For Rogers, the purpose was for the therapist to check his or her understanding. For Gendlin, the purpose of listening is to support the client in checking within, checking with that inner "something." The words Rogers used, to express the therapist's attitude toward the client, now fit the client's attitude in offering words and images back to the "felt sense." "Is this the way it is in you? Am I catching just the color and texture and flavor of the personal meaning you are experiencing right now? If not, I wish to bring my perception in line with yours."

Presence
There is no disagreement over this key insight: Attitude is far more important than technique. Rogers was appalled when his non-directive approach was reduced to a technique of reflection of feelings, and fought back by putting forth empathy as an attitude or "way of being" rather than as anything one "does." Edwin McMahon and Peter Campbell, beloved and influential Focusing teachers who emphasize the caring and gentle aspect of Focusing, have this to say:

Remember, the greatest gift we give to someone whom we accompany in Focusing is a caring presence that is non-manipulative. Technique can be very helpful, but in the long run is of little consequence if this presence is missing. (1991, p. 21-22) There is no question that listening (reflection) should not be done as a technique, but as an expression of an attitude of presence with and for the client. Having said that, however, we can acknowledge that listening is an unequalled way to express the attitude of non-judgmental presence.

A safe and steady human presence willing to be with whatever comes up is a most powerful factor. If we do not try to improve or change anything, if we add nothing, if however bad something is we only say what we understand exactly, such a response adds our presence and helps clients to stay with and go further into whatever they sense and feel just then. This is perhaps the most important thing that any person helping others needs to know. (Gendlin, 1996, p. 11)

Expressing one's non-judgmental presence is the second purpose of listening.

The Inner Relationship

My own work, building on Gendlin's, has added one more purpose for listening. In addition to supporting the client in checking inside, and expressing one's own non-judgmental presence, the third purpose for listening is to support the client in facilitating and maintaining a positive inner relationship with "something" that is there for them.

Although Gendlin doesn't mention how reflecting can support this inner relationship, he has eloquently described the relationship itself:

The client and I, we are going to keep it, in there, company. As you would keep a scared child company. You would not push on it, or argue with it, or pick it up, because it is too sore, too scared or tense. You would just sit there, quietly. ... What that edge needs to produce the steps is only some kind of unintrusive contact or company. If you will go there with your awareness and stay there or return there, that is all it needs; it will do all the rest for you. (1990, p. 216)

This "unintrusive contact" that Gendlin describes is not even a checking; it is simpler than that. It is much more a "being" than a "doing." Even something inside that is "too sore, too scared or tense" to be checked with can still be kept company. And this is not only, and not primarily, the therapist's company. It is the client's "I" keeping company with the client's "it." (Gendlin, 1990, p. 222: "Focusing is this very deliberate thing where an 'I' is attending to an 'it'.")

We have spoken of the therapist's presence. The ability of the client to be with what is there, not merged with their experience but Present for it, can be called the client's Presence. (To distinguish the two, I will capitalize the word "Presence" when referring to the client's inner Presence with what is there for them. Barbara McGavin taught me to use the word Presence in this way, and showed me much about this beautiful concept. Much of my work with the Inner Relationship is also hers.)

Supporting this keeping company from Presence is the third purpose of listening.

The Purposes of Listening: Recapitulation

60

We can say that there are three ways that listening facilitates the Focusing process for the client. These correspond to three purposes for giving listening reflections.

(1) We listen to support the client in checking what comes with something inside, directly felt.
(2) We listen to offer our non-judgmental presence for the client's process.
(3) We listen to support the client in "keeping company" from Presence with something inside.

Definition: What is Listening?
The word "listening" has many meanings and many uses. In this paper, it is being used in its technical and specific meaning of making a statement that says back what the other person (focuser, client, partner) just said, exactly or in paraphrase, with no intention of changing or adding anything essential or of making any change in the other person's experience.

The listener says something back to the focuser (client) that has the purpose of "saying what they just said." It is in the form of a statement. Although it is usually not solely the exact words they said, even when the words are different, they are not different in essence. Nothing from the listener is being added, no opinions are being given, no change is being intended.

I would like to make the case that the process of listening does not include asking questions, not even by tone of voice. I am aware that not all Focusing teachers would agree with me on this, and I respect their opinion and their work. However, this has been my experience: that when the listening response includes a questioning tone, the focuser tends to be drawn out of direct contact with their process, towards contact with the listener. The classic instance is where the focuser has closed eyes until the listener's question, and upon hearing the question, the focuser opens their eyes and looks at the listener. Of course if the focuser wants to open their eyes and look at the listener, there's nothing wrong with that! But it's unfortunate if the focuser is drawn out of an inner contact which is otherwise going well, because the listener framed their reflection as a question. This goes against one of our main purposes for listening: that it facilitates the focuser in staying in relationship with something inside.

Furthermore, the nature of questions is such that, unless they are carefully framed, they can sound as if what is being questioned is not whether the word fits, but whether the focuser is right to feel or think the way they do. A striking example is this one from Kevin Flanagan's Everyday Genius:

61

Paula: No, I can't take it ... I just seem to fold inside ... I don't have the stomach for it anymore. Maybe I'm a coward.
Listener: A coward? (p. 153)

The Linguistics of Listening
When the purpose for listening evolved, so did the form. When the primary purpose of listening is to check the therapist's understanding of the client, as it was for Rogers, then sensitive paraphrases are better than word-for-word reflections.
Jan: And yet people say to me, "Jan, you're in your prime. You've got everything going for you!" And little do they know inside what I feel.
Carl: That's right. So that outside and to an observer, you are in your prime and you have everything going for you. But that's not Jan inside. Jan inside is quite different from that. (1986a, p. 145)

But once we are aware of Focusing, then at those moments when we sense that Focusing is happening in the client, repeating back the client's key words so that they can check them within becomes more important. In fact, the more the client is in contact with something inside, and the deeper and closer the client's contact, the more the exact words are needed and will even be insisted on by the empowered client.
C: I can hardly touch it. There is something and it is right here on the edge. I can hardly touch it; it is — I cannot want my mother, I can hardly say it.
T: You cannot want her. (Silence)
C: That is where I feel the noise like darts. (More silence.) It is real, real early.
T: It feels like a very early experience. (Silence)
C: I cannot want anything. (Silence...) This needs to rest and it cannot rest. If it lets down and rests, it will die. It needs to keep its guard up.
T: There is such a big need and longing to rest and let down and ease; but somehow also this part of you cannot rest. It feels that it will die if it stops being on guard. (Silence...)
C: Maybe it could, if I could trust something.
T: It could rest if you could trust something.
C: No, no. MAYBE it could rest if I could trust something.
T: It is important to say 'maybe'. "Maybe it could rest if I could trust something." (Gendlin, 1990, p. 219)

But of course the client is not always in deep, close contact with something inside. What then? In the rest of this paper, we will explore linguistic forms that help listening do its work and accomplish its three purposes. It should go without saying that any talk about linguistic form assumes that the listener's attitude is one of unconditional presence, or at least of acknowledging any parts of him or herself that are not able to be unconditionally present. Tone of voice

and pace/timing are also important, and not in the scope of this paper.
There are those who would say that, once the listener's unconditional attitude is
in place, it doesn't matter what words are used. I don't agree. Just because
attitude and presence are more important than words doesn't mean that words are
unimportant. There are those who feel that conscious attention to word choice
changes the relationship between listener and focuser, makes the listener
somehow inauthentic or a manipulator. I respectfully disagree. I can understand
the problem, and in some instances I share it: I have a longstanding dislike of
techniques of rapport-building (as in Neuro-Linguistic Programming) where, for
example, the therapist consciously breathes along with the client. I believe that,
in most cases, helpful tone of voice, pace, and timing of listening responses can
be trusted to arise naturally out of the listener's presence. But when it comes to
words, I feel we can be conscious of making facilitative word choices and be in
an attitude of presence with the client. The suggestions that follow are offered in
this light. They are by no means a complete list of all types of facilitative
listening forms, but are simply those which I find most interesting from a
linguistic point of view.

The Power of "Something": Pointing to Felt Experience
The focuser needs to sense into a place inside. When the listener's response
includes the word "something" used appropriately, this helps to make a place
inside the focuser that can be sensed into. The word "something" is an invitation
to be aware of a place which is already implicit; therefore the phrase "make a
place" in the previous sentence isn't quite right. At the same time, until the word
"something" points to the place, there's a way in which it isn't there yet. So both
are true.

How may we help a person to find and attend to that unclear edge in the border
zone between conscious and unconscious? One way to do so is to respond in a
pointing way toward an unclear "something." (Gendlin 1996, p. 47)

C3: I had a dream... I was alone with this guy, ah (silence)... and the dream was
real nice, it was a real nice relationship. When I thought about it next day I
thought, why don't I have a real one! I don't think he could really see anything
wrong with me. I was also thinking why I was absent in school so much. When
it comes to the end of the line I don't have a paper, I hold back. I get jittery and
then I pull away from it.
T3: You're saying there is *something* similar about those two things.
C4: Yeah, I have all these excuses about why I never do my best, uh —
T4: You come right up to the line and then *something* holds back.
(pp. 41-42, my italics)

Gendlin points out that the therapist could have reflected without pointing at a "something." T3 could have been "not handing papers in is like not getting with a man" — which surely qualifies as understanding what the client is saying. So this "pointing at a something" is a special Focusing move, informed by our awareness of how powerful it is to be at an unclear edge, a fuzzy not-yet-fully-described experience that is like a door into unfolding.

F: There isn't anything else I can do about it.

L: There's something in you that feels there isn't anything else you can do about it.

F: I don't want to go anywhere near it.

L: There's something in you that doesn't want to go anywhere near it.

Saying Back What is There; Not Saying Back What's Not There

It is obvious that the focuser can only feel into what is there for them; they can't feel into what is not there. Yet people talk all the time about experiences that they are not having, or not able to have.

"There's also something vague. I can't get what it is."

"I don't know where this is coming from, but I'm getting the sense that this part of me needs support."

"I'm not sure how to describe this feeling in my throat."

I would suggest that the way to support the Focusing process is to say back what is there, but leave out what is not there.

F: There's also something vague. I can't get what it is.

L: You're sensing something there that's vague.

F: I don't know where this is coming from, but I'm getting the sense that this part of me needs support.

L: You're getting the sense that this part of you needs support.

When the focuser doesn't use a word to refer to what is there, and yet something clearly is there, the listener can supply the word "something" to point to what is there.

F: I'm not sure how to describe this feeling in my throat.

L: You're sensing something there in your throat.

Reflecting Fresh Air

Whatever is fresh, new, something stirring, always needs support. The listener gives that support simply by saying that part back.

The following sequence occurred in a partnership session between two experienced focusers:

F: [Something here] needing to rest. And needing privacy. That's strong — doesn't want to be seen, or to relate.

C: It doesn't want to relate, or be related to.

F: It could be gently touched, but doesn't want talking. Doesn't want to have to respond.

C: You're aware of something there that could be touched, just that much is possible. Gently touched.

The Companion, Chris McLean, had this to say afterward: "I chose this part to mirror — the touching — even though the last thing that the Focuser had said was 'Doesn't want talking. Doesn't want to have to respond.' I think I sensed a movement in the whole thing, a movement forward. We had already been with the part that didn't want to respond, and here was this new thing, so I reflected just that."

Often, the "fresh air" can be found, not so much in the literal words the focuser says, but rather in the positive implications of a negative statement. This would be a sentence which means the same as what the focuser said, a paraphrase, but with no "not" in it. (By the terms "positive" and "negative" I am pointing only to a linguistic fact, whether or not there is a "not" in the sentence. I am not otherwise evaluating the statement.)

F: It doesn't know how to settle down.

L: It wants to find a way to settle down.

Here's another example, from the Focusing/Listening session given as the Appendix to this paper:

A: ... my awareness bounced over to the woman in the battlefield to invite her to sense what she would want as well. And she said "Don't rush me. I'm not finished yet."

B: Yeah, she has something she needs to do first. She's not finished with something.

Here the listener re-phrased "Don't rush me. I'm not finished yet." as "She has something she needs to do first." This illuminated the positive (i.e. containing no "no" or "not") inside the negative. The listener then reflected the focuser's words more closely ("She's not finished with something") to make sure they were heard.

Disidentification

I cannot overemphasize the importance of disidentification. We've spoken already of the power of the Inner Relationship and the focuser being in Presence with what is there. Disidentification is the first key that opens this big realm of inner Presence.

Gendlin says, "Focusing is this very deliberate thing where an 'I' is attending to an 'it'." Yet people often speak, and experience themselves, as all "I."

"I want to run."

"I'm afraid I'm never going to get over him."

"I want to go and I don't want to go."

"I don't seem to like myself very much."

There is no "it" in any of these sentences, and we don't know whether there is an unspoken "it" in the person's awareness — perhaps not. Without an "it" in awareness, Focusing is often harder, so a listener can facilitate Focusing by offering an candidate for "it," for the focuser's consideration.
Here is one way to do this:
F: I want to run.
L: There's a wanting to run.
"I want" has become "there's a wanting," and thus more of an "it" to feel into.
Our favorite word, "something," offers another way:
F: I'm afraid I'm never going to get over him.
L: Something in you is afraid you're never going to get over him.
When the focuser is clearly experiencing parts, they will probably appreciate receiving a reflection using "a part of you."
F: I want to go and I don't want to go.
L: Part of you wants to go and part of you doesn't want to go.
This clear separation of parts can be especially valuable when the focuser is locked in an inner struggle.
F: I don't seem to like myself very much.
L: There's something in you that doesn't like something in you very much.

Fritz Perls and the Empty It
People who've studied with Perls (father of Gestalt Therapy) or his students are sometimes taken aback at our Focusing love for this little word "it." Perls is famous for insisting that his students own their feelings, using the word "I" in places where they'd previously said "it." "It's sad" would become "I'm sad," "it's depressing" would become "I'm depressed," and so on.

I've had people say to me, "I'm working hard to own my feelings, and now you seem to want me to go back to saying 'it' again!" My response is that I'm happy they've learned to own their feelings — and now I want them to go, not back, but even further. The disowning "it" which Perls and others so rightly dislike is not the "It" of Focusing.

In the structure of the English language, every sentence requires a subject. Sentences which describe processes where there is no actor are given "empty" subjects: "It's raining," "It's dark out." The "it" here means nothing, refers to nothing. These sentences would be just as meaningful without it — "Raining." "Dark out." They just wouldn't be grammatical.

We speakers of English have made use of this empty "it" to distance ourselves from feelings and opinions, making them seem as impersonal as the weather.
"It's interesting."
"It's scary."

"It's impressive."
"It's overwhelming."
"It's depressing."
Each of these sentences gives the illusion that it is not about the speaker, but about some condition outside of the speaker. I can say that the book was interesting, the movie was scary, the bridge was impressive, the task was overwhelming, and the loss was depressing. When, actually, in every case I am speaking of my own feelings: it's I who is interested, scared, impressed, overwhelmed, depressed.

But this empty "it" is not the Focusing "It," because the Focusing "It" refers to something felt in inner experience. It is not empty. It refers. So if I start by saying "It's scary," then own the feeling by saying, "I'm scared," I would then move in a Focusing way to sense the scared in my body, and say, perhaps, "In my stomach I'm sensing something that's tight. It's scared." "It's scary" — empty it — has become "I'm scared" — owned feeling — has become "It's scared" — something to be with in a Focusing way.

We certainly never want to go backwards, and turn a Focuser's "it" back into an identified "you."
F: "This place in my stomach is angry."
Not recommended: L: "You're angry."
Preferable: "That place in your stomach is angry."
"Something" is Alive
Earlier, we quoted from a client session cited by Eugene Gendlin (1990), as an example of how the therapist follows the client's words very closely if the focuser is in deep contact with something inside. But there was one place in this example where the therapist varied the client's words slightly and significantly.
C: I cannot want anything. (Silence...) This needs to rest and it cannot rest. If it lets down and rests, it will die. It needs to keep its guard up.
T: There is such a big need and longing to rest and let down and ease; but somehow also this part of you cannot rest. It feels that it will die if it stops being on guard. (Silence...)
What the listener has done has somehow enlivened the part. Where the client said, "It will die...", the listener responded, "It feels that it will die." "It will die" could have been an outer description, an objective assessment. The listener responds from inside a "living It," from the Its own point of view.

As a Focusing session continues, the "something" in awareness often takes on more and more of the qualities of being alive. Ideally the listener recognizes that this is happening and responds in a way that supports the aliveness.
F: It's tired. It doesn't want to speak.
L: It's letting you know that it's tired and doesn't want to speak.

Who's Saying It?

Linguistic theory tells us that every sentence uttered is situated in time and place and oriented as to its speaker and hearers. This is why we can use relational words like "I," "you," "now," "then," "here," etc. and have them understood, even though "I" refers to me when I use it and to you when you use it. If we don't know who said the sentence (or where or when), then we don't know what or whom these relational words refer to.

The most obvious way this applies to the linguistics of listening is that we change these relational words when we say back the focuser's sentences.

F: Something in me is angry.

L: Something in you is angry.

F: I'm sensing a heaviness right here.

L: You're sensing a heaviness right there.

Although, since we're speaking at the same time as the focuser, we don't need to change their time-reference words.

F: Now it's starting to change.

L: Now you're sensing it starting to change.

There are some practitioners of listening who do not change the other person's words at all. To me, this sounds quite strange, but I can understand it if I imagine the listener is saying back the focuser's words in quotes.

F: Something in me is angry.

L: "Something in me is angry."

It's quite true that sometimes the focuser says words that sound so powerful and meaningful that we hesitate to change them, even an iota. When that happens, I prefer to make the quote explicit, by saying something like, "What comes there is..." or "The words that come are..."

F: I never have to put up with that again!

L: The words that come are: "I never have to put up with that again!"

Whenever the listener feels it would sound odd to repeat the focuser's words, it's usually because, without any preamble, it would sound as if the listener agrees with what the focuser is saying. Rather than reports of body sensations or emotions, these are usually value statements. There's rarely an "edge" for sensing into in a statement like this. Often it issues from a part that would like to close a door, rather than open one. So it is helpful if the listener can point to that part, the one who is speaking, using our favorite word for pointing to edges: "something."

F: There's nothing that can be done about people like that.

L: Something in you is saying: "There's nothing that can be done about people like that."

Whenever it is clear that the words are coming from a part, from something inside, not from the focuser's "I," it's especially helpful to put the focuser's words in quotes and state who is saying them. "Something in you is saying" is generally useful if the part is unidentified. But sometimes you can make a pretty good guess who is speaking.

F: I'm feeling this part of me that's so . . . angry, I guess. Like a little kid who hates everyone.

L: That part of you feels like a little kid who hates everyone.

F: Just get away from me!

L: It's like that kid is saying, "Just get away from me!"

Presence Listening

We've said that the third purpose for listening is to support the focuser in "keeping company" from Presence with something inside. We've talked about the importance of disidentification, and how listening responses can support the focuser in remembering that they are not their anger, not their fear, not their tightness, not their judgment, not any of their temporary states.

But what is the focuser, if they are not their temporary states? Barbara McGavin and I call this Presence: the state of being able to be with anything, without taking sides, without judgment or agenda. Qualities of Presence include: Compassion, allowing, spaciousness, openness, acceptance, patience, gentleness...

Gendlin calls this "being friendly toward a felt sense, and the friendly reception of whatever comes from it (1996, p. 55). McMahon and Campbell call it the "caring-feeling-presence" (p. 11). Clearly it's something that helps Focusing happen. How can a listener help engender Presence?

What the listener can do is to reflect the focuser's presence with what they are saying, making it explicit. Each time the focuser describes something they are experiencing, it is understood that they are experiencing it, sensing it. By making that sensing explicit, the listener confirms, supports, and deepens the focuser's experience of Presence. We recommend doing this with the words "You're sensing...", though "You're aware of..." "You're noticing..." and in appropriate cases "You're realizing..." will work also.

F: This place in my stomach is clenched with anger.

L: You're sensing that place in your stomach is clenched with anger.

F: I've got a tight band across my chest.

L: You're sensing something in your chest like a tight band.

F: Oh, I see! This part believes that no one can ever help.

L: You're realizing that that part believes that no one can ever help.

When the focuser doesn't feel Compassionate or patient or accepting toward some part of themselves, they are not in Presence. Yet Presence is always there, available, behind the temporary identifications. So if the listener reflects what

the focuser says as if they were in Presence, it functions as a kind of subtle invitation — which, like all invitations, can be refused — to find Presence again.
F: I don't like this heavy part of me.
L: You're sensing a part that feels heavy, and you're sensing another part that doesn't like it.
F: I'm angry!
L: You're sensing something in you that's angry.
F: No, I'M angry!
L: Oh, YOU'RE angry!
Combining this "you're sensing" with "something in you" is what Barbara McGavin and I call "Presence Listening." The effect is often to illuminate that two parts are there, and to offer to the focuser to opportunity to acknowledge and be with either or both.
F: This part needs to change quicker.
L: You're sensing something in you that's needing this part to change quicker.
F: It's scary.
L: You're sensing something in you that's feeling scared, and something that it finds scary.

The Power of Listening
My personal belief is that listening is underused and underappreciated. I feel that when listening is used with sensitivity and skill, little or no guiding is needed, especially between Focusing partners (people who already know Focusing). When the companion uses all or mostly listening, and little or no guiding, this respects the focuser's process by staying out of its way, and it increases the focuser's sense of empowerment. It also decreases the companion's sense of taking responsibility for the session. For all that we've said about the gifts of skillful listening, it is still the focuser's session.

We could even speculate on the possibility that a need for guiding indicates a failure of listening. Or, to put it more positively, when listening is done well, there is less need for guiding.

An example of this occurred recently in a training session in my Center in Berkeley. The session seemed to go well, except for one moment when the focuser felt stuck and needed help from the teacher. In the discussion afterwards we went back to that moment and wondered if there was anything the listener could have done, with listening alone, to help at that moment. What we discovered was that there was little that could have been done at that moment, once the focuser felt stuck. But when we went back earlier in the session, to what came right before the stuck place, we saw that the listener had missed saying back a presently felt body feeling, and we could trace the "stuckness" directly back to that missing.

F: *I sense a kind of heaviness on my shoulders and upper arms.* Might be related to carrying something, kind of a burden
L: Something in you seems to be carrying some kind of burden.
F: Yeah, something in my shoulders and arms. That's where I sense it. I'm saying hello to that sense of carrying a burden and asking it to tell me more about that, what feels like a burden. (long pause) I'm sensing another part of me that wants to rush this process... (at this point the teacher offered help, inviting the focuser to sit with what was there with interested curiosity and sense from its point of view before asking it any questions)
Later the focuser agreed that if the italicized phrase had been said back, something like: "You're sensing something like a heaviness in your shoulders and upper arms...", it would have helped her stay more directly in contact with the felt sense, rather than moving into her thoughts about it.

In an earlier draft of Eugene Gendlin's book about Focusing and psychotherapy, there is a beautiful metaphor about listening. I haven't been able to find it in the published book, so I'm quoting it here from the draft:
[Listening] is something like adding to the motion of a fly-wheel. The wheel is already moving and you want to add movement to it. Therefore you don't stop it first, so that you can push it. You give it short spurts that can go with the movement it has already. (p. 372): How They Come and How to Help Them Come," in Client-Centered and Experiential Psychotherapy in the Listening is like touching an already turning wheel, in the same direction that it's moving. Nothing dramatic appears to be happening. Yet a space is created for the greatest of all human miracles: how much more happens when we allow what is to find its own unfolding, than when we try to make something happen.

References
Flanagan, Kevin. 1998. Everyday Genius: Focusing on Your Emotional Intelligence. Dublin, Ireland: Marino Books.

Gendlin, Eugene. 1984. "The Client's Client," in Client-Centered Therapy and the Person-Centered Approach, eds. Levant and Shlien. New York: Praeger.

Gendlin, Eugene. 1990. "The Small Steps of the Therapy ProcessNineties, eds. Lietaer, Rombauts, and van Balen. Leuven, Belgium: Leuven University Press.

Gendlin, Eugene. No date. Experiential Psychotherapy. Draft, distributed by The Focusing Institute.

Gendlin, Eugene. 1996. Focusing-Oriented Psychotherapy. New York: The Guilford Press.

McMahon, Edwin M. and Peter A. Campbell. 1991. The Focusing Steps. Kansas City, MO: Sheed & Ward.

Rogers, Carl. 1980. A Way of Being. Boston: Houghton Mifflin.

Rogers, Carl. 1986a. "A Client-Centered/Person-Centered Approach to Therapy," in Psychotherapist's Casebook: Theory and Technique in Practice, eds. Kutash and Wolf. Reprinted in The Carl Rogers Reader. Boston: Houghton Mifflin, 1989.
Rogers, Carl. 1986b. "Reflection of Feelings," Person-Centered Review, vol. 1, no. 4. Reprinted in The Carl Rogers Reader. Boston: Houghton Mifflin, 1989.

Appendix: A Listening Session
A: OK. So I'm bringing my awareness into my body. And I'm sensing, like there's a person inside me, a part of me. I feel her as a she, who feels — the word is shell shocked, and also — there is a sense of her coming back, almost like maybe even from a coma or emerging from a long period of illness (mmm) still weak and then coming out into a place where, uh, she's looking around and there's a sense of something she doesn't even understand. Other things are kind of coming at her dragon-like like why didn't you do this yet? Why didn't you do this yet? And, uh, a little bit of a sense of being overwhelmed and behind and weak and confused — and I m just sensing what really feels central in all of that. (long pause) Her — it's interesting, her emotion isn't fear or guilt or any of those things. She's really — bemused maybe more than confused. Like an innocent. She has an innocence about her (uh huh).

B: You can sense that there's an innocence about this girl, female, woman, person.

A: Yeah, she's a woman, she's not a child. She's walking through a battlefield where the battle is over. She's touching pieces of cannon and bodies and things. Touching them with an innocence as if she were touching flowers. Like, just curiosity.

B: You're seeing her walking through this battlefield, touching the dead, cannons, whatever with a kind of innocence like they are flowers, curiosity.

A: Makes me remember a poem I wrote when I was sixteen or something. I don't remember it but the first line was: And if we pick our way through a battlefield...

B: Yeah, that comes there.
A: And tears are here.

B: You can sense tears.

A: (long pause) So many of my clients have been working lately with a part that's stunned with pain and another part that's anxious with moving forward with life. And so I'm looking, or beginning to get a sense of a counterpart that's anxious.

B: Uh huh, so you're starting to sense a counterpart right there that's anxious.

A: That says "Come on, we can't take any more time with this, we have to get moving!"

B: Yeah, you're hearing it say, "Come on. We don't have any time for this. Got to get moving!"

A: And that woman in the battlefield, she can't be hurried. There's no way. She doesn't even hear, or she vaguely hears those urgings to move but they hardly penetrate. She's much more involved in what she's doing.

B: Mm hum, you can sense how she can't be hurried. She's involved in what she's doing. The other voice is just... she hears it but just barely.

A. Mm hum. So I'm saying to the other voice, "Yes, I know you're scared. You're scared something will be damaged or fall apart if attention isn't paid."

B: You're really letting it know you hear how it's scared.

A: (long pause) That part, yeah, it's beginning to show me its wanting as well, at least one level of it. It's like there's a yearning, it feels like that part is carrying that right now. A yearning to express our messages into the world and have them be heard there. Like even, I have, even as I do this session there's something in me that says, "You know this could be animated!" (laughter) Technology isn't that hard anymore and we could animate lots of these typical parts and counterparts and people could really relate to that. And that would really help. And it's like (uh huh) [big sigh] a sense of a big, at least that part feels, a big gap, a distance between what I feel capable of ...

B: Yeah, you can sense how this part is carrying the longing for all the potential...

A: Yeah, the gap between the reality and the potential feels really big (yeah) right now. And this part feels like one of the problems is this woman in white who's looking...

B: It's like from its point of view this woman is the problem, or a problem (one of the problems, right) in between the potential and where you are right now.

A: Right. And I want to just acknowledge the feeling of the gap and acknowledge to that part that it's so much wanting that to change that it's so much trying to figure out what the problem is.

B: Mm hum. Yeah, you're really letting it know you can sense how much it's wanting to reduce that gap.

A: Yeah. Huh. The way you said that made me want to ask what having a reduced gap would feel like.

B: Mmmm.

A: And I felt that for just a moment, and my awareness bounced over to the woman in the battlefield to invite her to sense what she would want as well. And she said "Don't rush me. I'm not finished yet."

B: Yeah, she has something she needs to do first. She's not finished with something.

A: Yeah. And saying that way, and hearing you say it back that way, she shifts a little. She was looking really dazed and again, what was the word at the very beginning? Shell-shocked. And now she looks more purposeful. (mmm) She has something she needs to do. That's right. (uh huh) And she's wanting to do it and not be rushed, because it wouldn't be right to rush. (uh huh) It can't be done in a rush.

B: Uh huh, whatever this is that she needs to do it can't be done in a rush and you can sense there's a purposeful quality to her now. (yeah) Sounds like there's a kind of strength there.

A: Yeah, I feel — well I'm feeling really touched. and not only by that but I also went over to the other one (uh huh) and it shifted too (ah) 'cause in the presence of her purposefulness, it's sensing that its purpose right now is to just hold the intention and hold the awareness of the potential and it's feeling good and proud that it has that purpose.

B: Yeah...
A: All of that is touching me. [tears]

B: You can sense how that other part is holding the potential. It is like a container for it - or something like that.

A: Yeah, yeah.

B: And it's feeling proud (yeah) that it has this purpose.

A: Yeah, it's feeling much more able to be patient.

B: Uh huh. As it senses her purposefulness, her needing to do something.

A: Yeah, and again as I feel its willingness to be patient, I feel touched. Tears come. (yeah) I feel touched by the willingness to carry the purposes of both these parts. (yeah) Oh, fabulous.

B: Yeah, you're sensing touched by the willingness to carry the purpose of both these parts.

A: Yeah... we're coming to a good stopping place.

B: And there's about two minutes.

A: [big sigh] Yeah, I think it's the whole thing about being heard that this anxious part shifted from being anxious (yeah) to being honored. Its job is to remember the potential. That's still true, it was true before. But when it's heard then it shifts from being anxious about remembering the potential (uh huh) to being honored to remember the potential. Cool.

B: And it doesn't have to be pushy.

A: Yeah, yeah. And it doesn't have to — there's some kind of being part of a larger team and it doesn't have to feel alone (yeah) and the "anxious" comes from feeling like nobody is going to hear it.

This article appears in The Radical Acceptance of Everything, by Ann Weiser Cornell, PhD and featuring Barbara McGavin (Calluna Press; 2005).

Creating Caring Feeling Presence
Kathy McGuire, Ph.D.

"… the most essential aspect for successful…Focusing [is] creating a positive attitude, inside of yourself, for whatever might arise during a Focusing turn. This is The Focusing Attitude.

Empathy, Congruence, and Unconditional Positive Regard

It is also the essential attitude which you convey to a Focuser when you are being a Focused Listener:
"I am here for you, without judgment. I am happy to receive anything that comes up inside of you, without criticism. I will set aside my own reactions, judgments, own experiences and be here as a Caring Feeling Presence simply to listen to and to give back to you your own experiencing." It is a necessary component of the "empathy, congruence, and unconditional positive regard" which Carl Rogers defined as the crux ingredients for the healing relationship.

Leaning in with Tenderness: A "Caring Feeling Presence"

Once I was having a prolonged argument with another Focusing Trainer at a workshop I was teaching. I kept emphasizing going with the tears and anger, letting them be experienced. He said it was sufficient to work his feelings through in his imagination, that he did not have to say them out loud, that he did not need to feel them. Then, in a Focusing turn, the Listener used his name: "So, H, you are saying---" "So, H, what mattered was" My friend reported to me that just hearing his name created an intimacy that allowed him to feel his tears, and the deeper meanings in his experience, and how valuable that was to him--- The Listener had responded to him with a Caring Feeling Presence, and that had allowed the Focuser to turn toward his inner experiencing with the same attitude of unconditional love and self-Compassion.

Another time, I was the Focuser, being Listened to accurately but---well, it felt distant, too objective---I didn't feel "safe" becoming vulnerable in front of that distance. I asked the Listener to "lean in toward me more---be tender toward me---" When she did this, I was able to feel Compassion for myself, and to touch into the place of tears, the deeper meanings for me, the part of me that needed to be comforted in order to grow forward.

The Real "First Step" of Focusing: Self-Empathy, Self-Love

Pete Campbell and Ed McMahon, creators of the Biospiritual Focusing approach, always started their workshops by teaching The Focusing Attitude, which they called "A Caring Feeling Presence." They did not think anyone should begin to try out Focusing Instructions without first learning how to be kind and gentle with everything that arises inside.

And they knew that Focusers had to have this experience in a bodily-felt way, not just as an intellectual idea. Learning to take this Focusing Attitude toward oneself is a life-long learning for anyone wanting to "make peace" with all the different "parts" or "aspects" of themself.

Please try out their introductory exercise for finding a "felt sense," an "intuitive feel" for this kind of inner caring. It involves learning how it feels, in your body, when you are trying to show complete love and safety to someone. Then, turning that same loving attention, that Caring Feeling Presence, toward your own inner experiences:

A CARING FEELING PRESENCE INSIDE

"Take a moment to find a comfortable sitting position---
Loosen any clothing that is too tight---
And begin to come quietly inside by closing your eyes and starting to just notice your breathing---
Just noticing your breathing---going in---and out---in---and out---Let any sighs or deeper breathing arise naturally---
(one minute)

78

Now, notice your body, how it feels in the chair ---
Massage any spots that feel sore---
Massage your head---
Wrinkle up your face and stretch your jaw---and relax!!!!!
Make a few circles with your shoulders, bringing them up to your ears, around toward the back, and dropping them down---and repeating four or five times---
(one minute)
And now bring your attention inside, to the place where you find a "felt sense" or an "intuitive feel" when you are using Focusing, often in the center of your body, around the chest/heart area----
(one minute)
And now, imagine that you work in a hospital---
An infant has been left on the hospital steps---
Let yourself feel the impact of this situation in your body---
It is your job to pick up that infant and to convey to it, through your body, your way of holding it, that it is safe, that it is perfectly and truly wanted in this world. Imagine picking up that infant---
Now, imagine what you would do in your body to convey to that infant that it is perfectly safe, that it is truly wanted in this world---
(one minute)
Notice what you do in your body to convey this loving attention, without words-
(one minute)
Now, imagine turning that same kind of Caring Feeling Presence toward your own inner places, whatever they may be---
(one minute)
Bring to your mind times in your life went you felt loved and valued in this way. Look for particular places or people or animals or situations where you felt completely safe, completely wanted, basking in the warmth of loving attention--
(one to three minutes)
Choose one of these images/places/people/situations that could stand as such a strong symbol of this kind of safety that you could use the memory of it as an anchor or talisman to bring you to that sense of Caring Feeling Presence to your own inside experiences. We'll call that your Inner Nurturer---
(one to three minutes)
Now, look through your life and store of memories and images and see if you can find an image of a part of yourself that is now or was at some point very much in need of that kind of Caring Feeling Presence. It could be an Inner Child, yourself at a certain age or time of life. But it could be another kind of image: like "a wounded animal" or "a butterfly with a crumpled wing" or "a gangrenous leg---I just want to cut it off" or a particular physical tension (headache, tight jaw, stomach knot) that you often suffer from. We'll call that your Inner Woundedness---
(one to three minutes)

Now, imagine taking your Inner Nurturer and turning that Caring Feeling Presence toward your Inner Woundedness---
(one to three minutes)
Just spend some time seeing if you can touch your Inner Woundedness with that Inner Nurturing---
(one to three minutes)
And come back into the room when you are ready.

Things That Get In The Way of This Inner Attitude

This exercise is just a first step. You might have found that Inner Critical Voices arose while you tried this exercise ("This is silly!" "I don't have any weaknesses!" "It's too late. The past is the past," etc. In the next weeks, we will continue working with establishing a Caring Feeling Presence inside, and the things that can get in the way of that. Turning toward oneself, and others, with love and self-love, is a life-long learning! But we are starting today.

Experiential Listening

Nada Lou

There are two levels of experiencing:

Explicit experiencing, where you are one step removed from your actual feelings. You describe these feelings objectively.

Implicit experiencing, where you are in touch with actual feelings. It is in that latter state that change occurs, and this is what we want to be in touch with in **experiential listening**.

Immediate goal of experiential listening: get a feeling process going, stay with it, and allow it to deepen. Frequently people start to touch a feeling and then "whoosh" off, out of the feeling and onto the next story. You want them to stay with that feeling and let it deepen so that the implicit meaning can open up.

General Guidelines

The Listener needs to:

Have an attitude of
wanting to hear **exactly**
Say back the felt meaning
of what you heard

Listen for the next
response
If the person says that's not exactly right - acknowledge the correction and say
back again what you hear.
Please no -advice, judgments, arguing, rushing in to "fix it"

The Focuser needs to:

Check inside to become aware of felt sense
Check inside what feels comfortable to share and only share what feels
right for you
When the listener says it back to you, check inside to see if that is exactly
how you meant it
If you are uncomfortable with how you are being responded to, please tell the
listener
Please no -being too polite (not saying if it is not exact), accepting of advice,
judgments, letting listener rush in to fix it

It is your process - please value, respect, and cherish it

Role of the LISTENER

Needs to be aware when felt sense is emerging in focuser. To do this must be
aware of felt sense in self. You are keeping them company.

When the focuser is on track - stay out of the way

Hear and observe when a
person has a felt sense

Hear handle words
Watch when language becomes inadequate, or when the focuser starts to
describe emotions with visual or visceral expressions - e.g. "jittery", "pushed",
"glimmer", "it was washing all over me", "like everything inside me was
oozing out"

Often unclear "somethings" point to a felt sense
When someone has one of these- reflect it literally, using their own words - don't rephrase - then help them stay with it.

When felt sense is not there - help it form

Listen and reflect - hear what they say before directing to a felt sense.

If you feel they are talking on a very narrative level and could use to be deeper, you can make room for them to focus:
"Can you be with that feeling right now?" "Can you be silent for a minute and let yourself feel how you are in everything you just said?" "Just be silent a minute and see how all that feels inside."

Point to the source place where they could be feeling a felt sense - e.g. "that crying place", "a stirring", "an anxiety kind of thing" (NOT "you feel anxious")

If someone is using very specific, explicit word, you might make them felt sense like e.g. "I feel nervous" can be reflected as "You have a nervous kind of feeling inside" or "there is something nervous about that".

Use of something, to point to the process - what they feel might be very vague. Using "something" captures the felt-sensy quality. e.g. "a not-quite right -something about that conversation yesterday". Makes it concrete and validates it, even though it is vague.

Helping to make space for a feeling - "Can you stay with that for a moment".

Body reflections: "It looked like there was a smile, (tear, sight ...) there"

How does that feel for you right now? Check with that feeling and see if that's the crux of it for you. Really try to let your body sense the whole - all about that frustration, that anger, that.... Does that seem to cover it?

Whatever a person does with any of these interventions, just listen in response. The focuser might not be ready to be with a felt sense. Let it go, then try again later to bring them back to the felt sense.

When a felt sense emerges, you may want to use contentless statements designed to keep a person at a feeling place:

That's heavy
Let's make some space for that ..... you have a strong
feeling there
Wait a minute ... let's make sure we take that in
Aha! That's new ... let's be with that
Let's give it some room to breathe

Contentless statements designed to bring a client back to a feeling place

I am still sitting with that feeling "He won't respect my space." Could you go back and sense the flavor of that? ....
I am still back where you said "1 am so mad at her! Can you touch that mad again?" ...
Let's let that feeling you just expressed register: "1 want more out of my life". Go and see where you feel that in your body.

Use behavioral signs of where a person is

Check their face ... tightness, looseness, release
Use these signs to tell if you have reflected correctly, and if they are experiencing something.

Use linguistic signs

If a person is using "must" and "probably" they are not in contact with an experiential sense.

Point of access of Felt Meaning

Timing: Hear enough of the "story" so the person feels you understood it ... but point at the underlying implicit meaning, or guess at it so the person can contact it before s/he starts to say the story over and over.

Help the person to keep their critic off of them

Awareness of the critic, describe the critic.

Feel empathetic towards critic, console it if it's scared, anxious etc., but don't buy what it says.

Simple Listeners Responses

How does that feel for you right now ... check with that feeling and see if that's the crux of it for you now. Really try and let your body sense the whole ... all about that frustration, that anger ... does that seem to cover it?

Try to feel fine about it and then see what you feel in your body; Imagine yourself going ahead with no difficulties, and pay attention to what you feel inside.

Tap it lightly and see what turns up. Just sense it ... wait and see what comes from it.

You don't know what it all means, but you feel it "right there". If you keep your mind on that feeling it will probably tell you more why.

Selective empathy ... say reflectively the key words which seem to be handles for the body sense.

Timing is important ... if you wait too long to reflect, the felt sense may disappear.

Instead of responding to persoll's expressed meaning, respond to that in them, which is expressing it. Sense what that "awfulness" is that makes dependent so awful.

Emphatic imagining ... what might be there if a felt referent was there ... what might be there if a felt referent was there. Son says: "I really want to go there but I am so scared." Response: "Like there's a scared something stopping you" ..

Hearing the story and saying what you imagine the felt sense might be, if the person does not state it and can't seem to get in touch with it. Always be ready to let go of it if you are wrong.

Importance of having the focuser be on a solid ground

The focuser needs to feel on solid ground to be able to process a felt sense in a different way than it was processed in the original situation which may have evoked it.

Help focuser feel distance:

Back up to where the person feels on solid ground
Clear a space of whatever is so heavy and work on it from a distance.
Keep the whole of the felt sense in view rather than one intensely emotional part of it.
Have a focuser get into a good place first before s/he works on a very heavy issue.
Let them know you are keeping them company even in the place which hurts so much.

Helping another person Focus while talking

If you set aside a period of time when you only listen, and indicate only whether you follow or not, you will discover a surprising fact. People can tell you much more and also find more inside themselves, than can ever happen in ordinary interchanges.

If you use simple expression to show that you are following what they say, you will see a deep process unfold.

Some suggestions:
"Yes"
"I see"
"I lost you, can you say that again, please"
simple nod
aha

There are only two reasons for speaking while listening:
to show that you understand exactly by saying back what the other person had

said or meant,

or to ask for repetition or clarification.

You will be a good listener immediately if you:

Try following someone carefully without putting anything of your own in.

Never introduce topics that the other person didn't express.

Never push your own interpretations.

Never mix in your own ideas.

Give the speaker a truthful sense of when you follow, and when not.

"Can you say that another way? I didn't get it"
"I followed most of what you said, but could you tell me about ... some more"
"I got it!"

You must be truthful and indicate when you fail to follow.

"I got that, but can you repeat what followed"
"My mind wondered for a minute, could you repeat what you just said".

Absolute Listening

To show that you understand exactly:

It helps much more if you the listener will say back the other person's points, step by step as you understand them.

Make a sentence or two that gets at the personal meaning this person wanted to put across.

Use person's own words for the touchy main things.

87

People need to hear you speak -that you got each step.

Don't just let them talk - relate to each thing that they feel whether it's good or bad.

Don't try to fix or change or improve it.

Try to get the crux of it exactly the way they mean it and feel it.

Sometimes what people say is complicated check with them if you got it.

How you know when you are doing it right

People go further into their problems.
For example person may say" no .. it's more like that ... "
Whatever the person then says - take that in and say it back.
It is a step further. You have done it right.
Person may sit silently satisfied that you get it.
Person may show release, a relaxing ... a whole-bodied "Yes, that's what it is"

How you know when you did it wrong, and what to do about that

If nearly the same thing is said over again, it means the person feels you haven't got it yet.
See how focuser's words differ from what you said.

As you respond, focuser's face might get tight, tense, confused.
Stop and ask the person again how it is?

Focuser changes the subject (especially something less meaningful or less personal).
You can interrupt and say something like "I am still with what you were just trying to say about ... I know I didn't understand it right, but I want to."

Helping a Felt Sense form

Having made a point, and being understood, the person can focus before saying the next thing. Most people don't do that. They run on from point to point, only talking.

The focuser must keep quiet, not only outwardly but also inside so that the felt sense can form.

Some people talk all the time, either out loud or at themselves inside. Then nothing directly felt can form, and everything stays a painful mass of confusion and tightness.

Once a felt sense forms, people can relate to it. They can wonder what's in it, can feel around it and into it.

Some general instructions

The key concept of this process
Listening, responding, and referring to people's feelings just as they feel them.

Try some of them, one at a time, and then go right back to listening for a while.

Let person's process go ahead if it seems to want to move a certain way.

Don't insist that it move into what you sense should be next.

People often teach us how to help them.

Watch your person's face and body, and if you see something happening ask about it.

Non verbal reactions are often good signals to ask people to get them into a felt sense.

Feel easy about it if the person doesn't like what you are doing. You can change it, or you might not need to.

Give the person room to have negative reactions to you, and listen and say back what *they* are.

Does the voice sound angry? Discouraged? Insistent? What way were the words said?
Ask: "You sound angry ......   Are you? If answer is yes, ask what that is about.

When to help people let a felt sense form

When people have said all that they can say clearly, and they don't know how to go on.

When there is a certain spot that you sense could be gone further. When people talk round and round a subject and never go down into their feelings about it. They start to say things that are obviously personal and meaningful, but then go on to something else.

They tell you nothing meaningful, but seem to want to.

In this situation, you can interrupt the focuser and gently point out the way into deeper levels of feeling.

How to help a felt sense form

Always do the least amount first, and more only if that doesn't work.
There is a gradation of how much help people need to connect a felt sense.

Some people won't need any help except your willingness to be silent.

Don't interrupt silence for at least a minute.

The person may need one sentence or so from you, to make a pause in which a felt sense could form. Such a sentence might be to repeat the last important phrase - it might just point again to the spot.

Say the crux of it back.

You can tell them to do so more directly "sit with it a minute and feel into it further".
"Wait. Be a minute with your ... feeling." "Just feel it for a minute."

"See what is more in it. Don't think anything ... "

90

You can give some focusing instructions.

Questions directed to help felt sense form

You don't ever know what they feel
You only wonder and help them to ask themselves.

You can **form some open-ended** question for people.

All these ways require that the focuser stop talking, both out loud and inside.

One lets what is there come - instead of doing it oneself.

Tell them to **ask this question inwardly**, to ask not the head but the gut:

"Stay quiet and don't answer the question in words."

"Just wait with the question till something comes from your feeling".

"What really **IS this**?"

"What's keeping this the way it is?"

"How is that **whole** thing" - use it when everything is confused or when the focuser doesn't know how to begin.

How would it be different if it were all O.K.?

What ought it to be like?

What's in the way of that?

Person must feel what is there, to answer your question, if you put it this way.

PICK the two or three most important things the focuser has said, if you feel they go together in one idea.

Whatever you say or do -watch the person's face and respond to how you are in it affects the person. If you can't see than ask.

Make your statements **questions**, not conclusions. Direct your questions to people's **feelings**, not just their ideas. Invite people to go into themselves and see whether **they feel** something like what you say - or something else. Let go of your idea easily as soon as you see that it doesn't get into anything directly felt. Make sure there are stretches of time when you do total listening. If you interrupt with your ideas and reactions constantly, the basic focusing process can't get going. If the person is feeling into his or her problem do less of talking; if the person is stuck do more.

How to tell when a person has a felt sense

One has a felt sense when one can feel more than one understands,

when what is there is more than words and thoughts,

when something is quite definitely experienced but is not yet clear, hasn't opened up or released yet,

when the person gropes for words and evidently has something that is not yet in words.

Anything that comes in that way should be welcomed. It is the organism's next step.

It feels good to have something come directly from one's felt sense.

Even if one doesn't like what has come, it feels good.
It gives one a sense of process, feeing from stuck place.

How you can tell when it isn't working

When people look you straight into eyes, they aren't focusing inside themselves.

Say; "You can't get into it while you are looking at me. Let me just sit here while you go into yourself"'.

If people speak immediately after you get through asking them to be quiet - they haven't focused yet.

If after silence the person comes with **explanation and peculations**,

ask how the problem feels.

If people say they can't let feeling come because ..... they are too restless, tense, empty ...

ask them to focus on that!

Notes on Listening # 1

Peter Campbell, adapted by Nada Lou

Why are we starting with Reflective Listening?

1. Basis of learning how to guide in focusing. It's not enough to just say the steps. People in deep places wander around. Reflective listening helps you stay with hem without derailing them.

2. It's the most common way you can get people to a focusing place out in the "real world".

What is Exact Reflective Listening?

Saying back exactly what the person said, using as much as possible, the same emphasis, though in your tonality. Not mimicking, which is imitating their tonality.

How is it Useful?

1. Tuning yourself to the other person, and away from your own head talk and mind reading. This is the base upon which all other kinds of listening are built.

2. It's a good form of listening :

a. when someone is in a deep place

b. when you are unsure of what's going on

c. when you made a different kind of reflection which leads the person off track.

3. Great training for Focusing guiding.

What are the "Rules" or "Obligations" of Both Sides?

1. Person listening: interrupt to keep the chunks manageable. Stop the Focuser to reflect when they are giving you too much.

2. Focuser: When it's not right, correct the Listener, either because they didn't say it right, or because it changed after they reflected it. If their reflection doesn't feel right in your felt sense, keep asking them to reflect it until it does feel right.

3. Person Listening: If you get corrected, go with correction.

Common Difficulties

Am I irritating the other person? Maybe. If they throw you out, stop.

I feel silly,
 because I am doing this.
 because I am having difficulty doing this.
 because this should be simple. It is not.

Further Guidelines for Healing Listening

James Iberg, Ph.D.

DO.
1. Quietly, with a minimum of your own thinking, listen to their words, but observe their situation, and observe their body language. Strive for an accurate and detailed impression of what the speaker is feeling.

DON'T.
1. Don't evaluate or react to what you are being told. Don't try to change how they are feeling. Don't try to find a solution for them.

DO.
2. Wait for a sense of how it is from inside the speaker's world to come to you before you say anything.

DON'T.
2. Don't talk just to be saying something. Silence often helps a person focus on their felt sense.

DO.
3. Express concisely, your sense of what the speaker is experiencing as he/she feels it internally and bodily.

DON'T.

3. Don't add or subtract or change any important feelings or ideas the person is expressing. Don't give advice. Don't interrupt the speaker's train of thought.

DO.

4. Welcome corrections. When you have misunderstood the speaker wore when he or she has thought of something else. Communicate your corrected understanding of what the speaker is telling you.

DON'T.

4. Don't argue with the speaker about what he/she is feeling, or dispute his/her corrections. Don't think of your listening as a test of your listening ability. An incorrect reflection made in good faith can be as useful as a correct one in helping the speaker focus on the felt sense.

DO.

5. Just to yourself, pay attention to the felt sense of your own reactions to what the speaker is expressing. Simply being aware of this in yourself and acknowledging it helps you to listen more effectively to this other person. Afterwards, if needed, you can use focusing to work with whatever is there.

DON'T.

5. Don't think about your reactions. Just notice the felt sense of them. Do your thinking about your reactions after the healing listening session.

Notes on Listening # 2
Nada Lou

Summary Listening

What is Summary Listening?
This is summarizing the main/most important pieces of what the Focuser said. As much as possible, use their key words. You may even reflect a key piece (phrase or sentence) exactly. This is not "saying back what I think they said" or "what I am most interested in". The most important pieces are defined as what they seem to care about most.

Notice their nonverbal emphasis. Signals that some emotion or meaning is present include: voice tone, voice emphasis, gestures, facial expression, posture.

When and how is Summary Listening useful?
It is most useful when someone is giving you a lot of content, or is more indirectly or occasionally touching deep places. It is useful in basic conversation, and where a person might resent or feel uncomfortable with Empathic Listening, which points directly towards feelings.

Summary Listening is also useful for focusing guiding. It trains you to notice the nonverbal cues that indicate importance. Often Focusers are silent, and nonverbal cues are important to allow you to stay with the person, to know when and how to come in, and when to stay out.

Summary Listening training is important in noticing what the listener believes is important. It's a way to get rid of your opinions, and a beginning to notice how the listener evaluates the content. There is as little interpretation as possible on your part.

As much as possible, you strive to have no opinions about what the listener is saying. You are simply staying with the person, walking with them, providing a friendly, caring feeling presence for them. Don't worry about your opinions.

Conflicting Parts and listening

Many people have conflicting feelings about what they are speaking. You hear them go from one side of an issue to another side. This is very common, perfectly normal, and more difficult and confusing for you, the listener.

The main point to remember is to reflect both sides equally. Don't chose one part over another! This takes some practice, first to notice and then do. However if you can accompany them in both sides of the conflict, you will be providing a major benefit to them.

"Getting it right" and Listening

It is important to keep in mind that you, as the listener, are only responsible for trying to get it right. The person talking is responsible for correcting you, if you don't.

We noticed a dramatic improvement in guiding, directly related to their improved ability to use exact reflective listening in guiding. This seems to be a major piece in training Listening.

A Checklist for Effective Healing Listening

Peter Campbell and Ed McMahon
Adapted by Nada Lou

1. Have I any hidden agenda in this relationship?

2. Do I mix myself into the other person's process?

3. Am I uncomfortable with silence?

4. Am I free enough in myself to allow this other person space to be and express him/herself?

5. Am I able to detect how the other person is "in" what he/she is saying?

6. Can I, as briefly as possible, say back what I sense as the personal meaning behind the other person's words and feelings?

7. Can I say back EACH felt meaning as I get it?

8. Do I know the difference between interrupting and supporting?

9. Do I know the difference between asking "open-ended" and "closed" questions?

10.   If I get *lost, do I go back to the last felt meaning I caught, repeat it and then ask the p*erson to go on from there?

11. What clues tell me I'm doing it right? What clues tell me I'm doing it wrong?

What is a Focusing Partnership?

From the Focusing Institute Website www.focusing.org

Many people all over the country have a focusing partnership. This means that they receive a half hour of attention from another person, and then they give the person a half hour of their attention, at least once a week at a regular time, either in person or on the phone.

Most people use the time to work on their main concerns that day, which might be inner experiences, their attempts to develop as people, or a difficult letter to write, the next thing to do in one's work, or whatever one finds uppermost.

Your partner offers no advice, no judgments, no comments. We have learned that people can go deeper and arrive at creative steps forward, if the listener refrains from adding anything in. Judgments, advice and comments express the person who is giving them, not the person to whom one is listening. Your partner will not say that your talk is superficial, or that it doesn't make sense, or that you are wrong, weak, or selfish, nor will the partner praise one thing and condemn another thing in you, or in what you say.

Partners need only say when they cannot follow you, so that you can rephrase what you said. But they pay close attention, and want to grasp every wrinkle of what you meant. There is no attempt to delve or probe or push more deeply into what you said. What counts is *what you meant to say*, what you *wanted* to convey.

Sometimes partners may repeat back and check: "You are saying ......". Of course they don't just repeat words. First they take in what you said, feel it in themselves, until that nodding "uhuh yes, makes sense", comes. *Only then* they might say it back, so that you can feel it and correct it, until it is exactly what you meant to convey. This "reflective listening" is a skill that anyone can learn. But most partners simply indicate when they have followed you, and when not.

You will find that you are with yourself in a way that is not possible most of the time, because other people usually need and demand something, or impact on you in some way. Neither can you sense yourself as deeply and easily when you are alone.

If you tell or even just quietly think about some business problem with your partner present, you will find that you can think about it more clearly. If you talk about something that makes you happy, you will find that it expands and makes you happier. If you tell about a personal problem, you will find that with this kind of safe attention you can stand to enter inside you, into "that unresolved thing, there." New steps and action-possibilities open where you were stuck before. This happens even if you were mostly quiet and only said that you were quietly working on something

Then you reverse roles. Now you are the listener. You are not expected to be wise, to know what the person should do, or how the person should live. You need not agree or approve what the person feels or says. You only take it in to sense whether you understand it. You ponder it a moment and find, yes, of course, you know what the person means to say. You are giving your full attention and presence, so that *that person's* meanings and feelings can emerge. These are often still puzzling and inarticulate inside the person, so that some silent times are needed for the person to sense them so that ways open to go further into them. You know this, so you don't mind sitting some minutes in silence. Out loud you say just the parts you want to say.

The partnership pattern

The person who is being listened to is in charge. My half of the time is for me. I need not use it for focusing or listening. I use it as I wish.

In my half of the time I might talk of some troubling situation. I might say everything I know about something, or only a little. I might talk of deep feelings without letting you know what situation they refer to. In that way I can be at my own edge without needing to share information. I say only what I am comfortable saying. I might focus silently some of the time, or all of the time, and want only your quiet attention. I might lay out the details of a work problem so that I can find how to go on with it, or I might tell you a story, talk about politics or some other topic I care about, read you a letter I received, or show you some photographs.

Partners assume the freedom to be quiet or to say only what they want to say. Therefore, when my turn begins, I feel how inviting my time is -- it is open just for me. I might know immediately what I need, and just start. Or, I might spend some minutes, scanning, sensing what I might like. I would think: "I might talk of this..., no, perhaps that..., well, perhaps first focus quietly... Let me see..." I could have any of those things.

The time is divided exactly in half, and we keep track of the time. We keep exact track of time, and stop each other when the time is up. At first it may seem "mechanical" and inhuman to divide and keep track of time so exactly. But if that isn't done, one person takes more of the time, and the other is left to say politely, that it's OK. Then one partner has to become the more considerate person, or the more upset person, or the more important person, or whatever. Some people would constantly worry that they are taking too much time from the other person. Then there is no deep peace, and people stop as soon as they possibly can. Equality is a very deep thing which comes along with the seemingly superficial division of the time.

Who can be partners?

PARTNERSHIP presupposes that you know at least a little focusing and listening. If you don't have experience, you can get it in a number of ways:

- Read the six steps on this site, print them, and try them out with a friend.
- Read or watch videos about Focusing, and try it yourself or with a friend.
- Take a Level I or Level II workshop. They are offered all around the world.
- Have several individual teaching sessions with a Focusing Partnership Coach.
- After you know a little Focusing, you can use our on-line partnership program to set up your partnership and get it off to a good start.

The partnership pattern of dividing and owning half the time has now been used in many different kinds of settings.

It works best if the two people are not in a close relationship, but both really understand Focusing. People who are connected in other ways can be partners, although it is more difficult.

Two people who work together may use the partnership pattern at lunch or on the way to work. An exchange even of 10 minutes each way can help reduce stress at work.

A business person can focus and find the next step on a work problem and arrive at work already knowing how to tackle it. A social worker or a nurse can receive some time just for herself instead of only serving others all the time.

In college courses students can form pairs which meet for two hours outside of class. The class can be on any topic. The class changes from being the usual burden on the student. Now it is a source of life support. The students spend some of the time helping each other to understand the class topic and to write a better paper, but they know that their half of the time is their own. It just isn't partnership unless they can just as well use the time for anything but the topic of the course.

Can the person who is already my life partner also be my focusing partner? Some people have found it very helpful to add partnership time to existing love and friendship relations, but it can also backfire, or it can be quite impossible from the first moment. At any rate one must remain clearly aware that one cannot give or be given the neutral, open, pure attention that constitutes a focusing partnership. In a life partnership each person *can* listen and feel the other's meanings, but never without *also* feeling how one's own life is affected by them.

Is it safe?

Can you entrust yourself to someone who knows no more than you do, perhaps far less? Trust may certainly develop, but in a partnership you don't *en*trust yourself to anyone. You stay in charge of your own life and your own process, *of course*.

People cannot really be displaced from the driver's seat of their lives. In a Focusing Partnership, each person is well aware that the other is no authority. No money is exchanged. No one is the expert. Anything stupid is easily recognized as such, and discarded. From a partner you will not put up for ten minutes with what many patients go through for years with credentialed professionals. In a partnership, long before it could hurt someone, the person changes partners, or simply does not come to meet the partner anymore.

Partnership is not mutual therapy. Partnership is a new pattern. A partnership is a special relationship in which you can be safe to be yourself. It is not based on sympathy or shared topic of interest. It's not based on any content at all. It is based on sharing a certain kind of process together. Your work life and your inner life can have company and not get stepped on. You must make your own assessment about the value to you of any particular partnership. Sensitivity, confidentiality, and a deeply felt ethics usually develop in nearly every partnership.

Training

We find that *training* is quite essential for focusing and listening, but it doesn't matter how one comes by that training. It is quite possible for a trained focuser or listener to train a partner, informally. In fact, informal training is one of the best kinds. There is no pretension and no pressure; one gives the other person what one knows, bit by bit, at appropriate times, as focusing and listening happen.

One can show a new listener a few times, just what to say: "Now I need you to say back to me: 'You feel unsure of what to do because...'" Then, later, when the listener tells me something intrusive, I just say "No, don't take me away from what I'm working on. Let me go further into it. Just say "that scares you." The listener feels a little artificial saying "That scares you", but when I then go silently into myself and come out with more, the listener is glad. The urge to tell me things soon drops out.

It is even easier to train a partner just enough so that we can do our own focusing. It only requires quiet attention. Then we can focus in our own time. We can teach focusing by giving small focusing instructions in the partner's half of the time, when that is welcome.

The Focusing Institute and Focusing Institute trainers around the world offer workshops and individual sessions to train people in Focusing and Listening skills.

Do I have what it takes to be someone's partner?

107

Two things are required -- but every human being has them. One requirement is the capacity to shut up -- to keep quiet and to be unintrusive company. When the other person is talking, we control any urge to impose something. It means letting go of our many excellent ideas, interpretations, suggestions, and our desire to give friendly reassurances, or to tell what we did in a similar situation. And when the other person is quiet, it means keeping our attention on the person without hearing anything interesting.

The second requirement is to provide the company of a human being. You cannot fail to have this capacity, since you are a human being. It does *not* require a good human being, or a wise one, or any special quality. It does not require some special way of being or showing one's humanness. Just you, there.

Listening Exercise
Diana Marder, Ph.D.

Week 2 Home Practice

The goal of this exercise is to experience the gift of simple attentive, accepting, listening, without the pressure of being "helpful", and to begin to break old habits, of questioning, advice-giving, etc.

Speaker

Choose something problematic that you would like to talk about for ten minutes. It needn't be very "deep" or serious. You needn't tell the whole background of the situation—you can just start in with what you are feeling or what is problematic for you. Try to notice what you are feeling in your body as you talk.

Listener

Just listen. No questions, no comments, no advice. Your goal is for the listener to feel accepted and understood. Make eye contact, use nods and brief comments (umhm, yes, sure….) to communicate attention and understanding.

After 10 minutes, switch places—the listener talks and the speaker listens.

Take a few minutes to discuss what this experience was like.

FOCUSING

LEARN FROM THE MASTERS

TRAINING MANUAL III

Focusing as a Spiritual Practice
Lucinda Gray, Ph.D.

In this third essay on "What is Focusing?" I will explain my view of Focusing as an advanced mental health practice, as well as a profound spiritual practice.

Consciousness expands through the practice of self-reflection. For thousands of years human beings have aspired to advanced states of consciousness through the practice of Hindu, Buddhist and Christian meditation and prayer. As a species, we have known that self reflection, watching the workings of ones own mind, is the only known path to enlightenment. Focusing is a newer method of self-reflection that has some advantages over earlier developments.

First, Focusing is a systematic self-reflective practice that provides a structure and steps that guide us through the process. Unlike the earlier traditions which initiate meditation but offer no framework to guide us, Focusing provides a specific step by step path that one can follow, making a practice of self-reflection easier for most people.

Secondly, Focusing is made possible through the application of the Focusing attitude. The process of Focusing requires that we give up self-blame and drop the judgment of our feelings, our injuries and human failings. Only with this basic position of blamelessness can Focusing work. When we can adopt the Focusing Attitude we can begin to see our problems, inadequacies, our failings

113

and our pain without self blame as a natural part of our human condition. This is the beginning of healing through self-empathy and self -forgiveness. What has been a painful injury or a feeling that we find unacceptable is now to be transformed into the relief of self-understanding and self-acceptance. This is the Focusing way of healing.

To be effective in changing consciousness Focusing must be practiced regularly as you would practice meditation. In this way Focusing can work as a systematic exercise in empathy, Compassion and self-forgiveness. The regular practice of Focusing and the essential Focusing Matrix, also called the Focusing Attitude, helps establish an internal habit of non judgmental witnessing within which we see ourselves in the light of our full humanness, as vulnerable, injured, strong, competent and capable of even love and joy. Only when you stop judging yourself can you drop judgment of others. Now you begin to cultivate empathy for others as well as for yourself.

For thousands of years we humans have aspired to cultivate Compassion, recognized by the ancients as the essential characteristic of enlightened beings. Compassion is still the goal of Buddhist meditative practices. It is sympathy for and loving acceptance of all living things. It is the ability to hold all living things, yourself included, in a loving caring presence. Through the Focusing practice of empathy for yourself you cultivate capacity for empathy for others, the foundation of Compassion. If you can forgive yourself for your faults you can forgive others. In fact, not until you can forgive yourself can you forgive others.

Focusing is a Compassion practice. Focusing includes a special way of listening to ourselves and others with nonjudgmental blamelessness. We create a safe space for them by holding them in the light of Compassionate understanding. When they can be listened to in this gentle and caring way, they have a direct experience of empathy, which is healing in itself.

For the listener, the Focusing way of listening is an exercise in Compassion because we recognize experientially that, like us, every human being has within him/her the full range of all human emotions; fear, pain, hurt, shame, happiness, relief, love and joy. As the listener, you learn to make room for all of these, in yourself and others. Now none are unacceptable because they can all be allowed, experienced, understood and finally forgiven and even loved. All feeling states can be appreciated, enjoyed, and accepted as part of our essential humanness. This is the essence of Compassion.

In addition to being a direct path to personal growth and change, Focusing is a daily remembrance of self forgiveness. This daily practice forms the foundation of Compassion, thus Focusing is an advanced spiritual practice reinvented for the western mind, and available to us through spiritual application of the step by step structure of the Focusing process.

A Dozen Ways to Focus in Everyday Life

Diana Marder, Ph.D.

Focusing doesn't always need to be a twenty or thirty minute formal session. Sometimes the most value comes from these little ways of Focusing on-the-fly as the occasions arise. Over time you may find yourself approaching yourself and your life in a gentler and more mindful way.

1. Avoid a fight.

Annoyed with your partner? Before spouting off, take some time to get in touch with the core of the issue. For example, if you are upset because you think someone insulted you and your spouse said nothing, a moment's Focusing may lead you to say, "I'm noticing something in me that feels very vulnerable and unprotected" rather than "How could you let him speak to me that way!" You'll probably get a much more supportive response.

2. Right yourself when you're off kilter.

Grumpy, out-of-sorts, irritable, or you don't-quite-know what? Take a deep breath, let your attention settle inside, sit quietly and attend to the fuzzy sense of something wrong. Give it at least a full minute to come into focus. Once you see what it is, you can give it some gentle attention till it shifts, or set it aside.

3. Guess wrong for more information.

Is your spouse, child or friend being inarticulate or silent but you know something's wrong? Give it your best guess..."You look like you're feeling a little sad...is that true?" Even if you're wrong, your attempt will help focus them on what s/he *is* feeling, and they'll probably open up a little.

4. Change your emotional wallpaper.

When you have a few moments free during the day, tune in inside, take a few breaths, and notice your overall feeling tone. Or clear a space and then tune in to what is left inside. Try to notice if there is a felt sense of "something" that is almost always with you, like a little sad, trying too hard, or feeling not-quite-adequate. Give it some gentle, accepting attention. Then try to imagine what it would feel like *not* to carry that felt sense. Just imagining even for a few moments, how it would be to not carry that, can be the first step toward positive change.

5. Take action.

Is there a chore you've been avoiding-even something as simple as a phone call? Put aside everything you already know about why you don't want to do it, and put aside all the lectures you give yourself about how silly this is or how you need to get it done. Now, imagine you are about to do that chore--maybe say to yourself "I'm going to do it right now." Now notice something that rises in your body that says "no". Is there a knot, a heaviness, a twist in your stomach? Find a word or two to describe it. Sit with it quietly, patiently, and *gently,* without judgment, for at least a minute. If nothing more unfolds, you can ask the [knot, etc.] "What makes this so... [your word]?", then go back to paying attention. It may take a few attempts.

6. Get fit, get organized, start a business.

Is there a project that you've been meaning to start, but somehow it never happens? Follow the same directions above. Some clues to look for...Is there a part of you that's not on board? A fear that needs to be heard? Something else you might neglect by using that time for your project? Your head thinks you want to but actually you really don't? Some way you aren't ready yet? Any of these and many other things can derail you from your goal. Remember; attend patiently, and without judgment, for at least one full minute. Be sure to fully receive whatever comes up. Next, if you like, you can ask what would be a small, easily doable action you can take, if you feel you want to.

7. Change your eating.

Do you feel you overeat for no good reason? The next time you have an urge to eat and are not really hungry, sit back, take a couple of nice deep breaths, and let your attention settle into your body. Feel your arms, your legs, and your back against the chair. Now let your attention settle down inside and notice what is there. At first you may notice nothing, or feel a bit uncomfortable. Be patient. Gradually you should get a clearer sense of the feeling or need behind your impulse to eat. Then you can find another way of satisfying it or go ahead and eat, but at least it will be mindfully.

8. Help a friend, student or colleague.

Sometimes when people are upset or confused they ramble on or talk in circles without getting much satisfaction or relief. Asking "What's the worst of all this?" often brings a felt sense; when this is articulated, it's much more satisfying for both of you.

9. Make a decision.

Are you struggling with a decision? Try these approaches.

How does it feel to be making this decision? As usual, take a deep breath, settle into your body, and wait for a felt sense of "all about me and this decision. Back away from all the details and pros and cons and just sense into the whole of it. For example, you may find a fear of making a mistake. Give it gentle, patient attention.

Imagine you have already made the decision, and chosen alternative #1. Notice how that feels in your body. Give it time to develop and unfold. Now do the same with alternative #2.

Ask (your body) "What's in the way of my making this decision?"

Do you have an intuition or a gut sense that conflicts with your reasoning? Focus on your gut sense and give it time to unfold.

10. Look it up in the back of the book.

Usually we start Focusing with something problematic and stay with it through a number of shifts, until it feels clearer and better. But you can also go directly to the question "How would this feel if it was all O.K. or solved in just the right way? The emphasis is on *feel*; don't look for a rational solution. Once you get a felt sense of "all O.K.", stay with it a while, Then imagine bringing that feeling to your problem, or let an image come about how that applies to your problem.

11. Have a great day.

This is another form of "looking it up in the back of the book. Think of a quality you would like to experience today—or in any situation you are about to enter. Peace, joy, relaxation, connectedness...You might experiment with a couple, saying each word to yourself and seeing if it resonates in your body, before you choose. You can also do this if you're not quite comfortable in a situation—ask "What do I want to feel instead?" Once you've chosen your word, take time to let the felt sense fully develop in your body, maybe remembering a time you've felt that quality, if it helps. Go back and forth between the word and the felt sense, making sure they fit. Once the felt sense is gully developed, just saying the word should help bring back the body sense of the quality you've chosen.

12. Soften self-criticism

Do you ever tell yourself "It's stupid to be feeling (jealous, angry, hurt, abandoned...)". Or maybe you feel like you're too old to still be feeling this, whatever it is. Does saying this to yourself stop the feeling? Probably not. The next time this happens, try telling the critical voice "Come back when you've got something new to say; I'm busy right now". Then go back to whatever you were feeling before the Critic spoke, and Focus. Observe your feeling with interested, friendly curiosity. Sense how it sits in your body; sit with it through any shifts and changes. It may not go away, but you will learn something.

Focusing as a Doorway for Spiritual Growth

Lesley Wilson and Addie Van der Kooy

Having been regular Focusers for over 10 years, we are still amazed at how powerful a tool Focusing truly is. It has helped us with making important decisions in our lives, it has been pivotal in managing physical pain and it has become instrumental as a tool for healing, for example in facing deeply held traumas from the past. But above all, Focusing is for us a very simple and practical process for healthy spiritual growth which is firmly grounded in our physical bodies.

Focusing has enabled us to touch a directly felt experience of who we truly are and a directly felt connectedness and sense of belonging to some larger Life Process or Presence. Whether this is given a name - like Higher Power, God, Tao or the Great Universe - is not important. What matters is that we can actually feel and experience it directly in our bodies. For us, this has become the core of our journey and in this article we will explore the elements of Focusing that have opened the door for us into this experience.

But first, we want to acknowledge the pioneering work of two psychologists of religion, Dr Edwin McMahon and Dr Peter Campbell. Their work and teaching has been inspirational to us, providing profound guidance for our journey with Focusing. They recognized the significance of Focusing as a bodily grounded, practical pathway for healthy, spiritual growth. They trained and worked with

Dr Eugene Gendlin and have, for many decades, been researching, developing, teaching and writing about the spiritual dimension of Focusing. They use the term "Bio-Spirituality" to describe this body-based spirituality which goes beyond doctrine, religion, language and culture.

As they say in their book "Bio-Spirituality – Focusing As A Way To Grow"

> *"There are two critical issues in spiritual development...The first is to discover a holistic approach for letting go of the mind's omnipotent control as a prelude to allowing some broader wisdom within the entire human organism to speak. The second is to allow the unique next step that is "me" to emerge as an integral, harmonious expression of some Larger Process".*

Letting Be – "Letting go of the mind's omnipotent control"

Two words lie at the spiritual heart of Focusing: "Letting Be". They point to a bodily felt unconditional acceptance of what is there. When we listen to a place inside that hurts, for instance, the quality of our presence is not the usual one of fixing or trying to make it feel better. Rather, we are willing to let it be exactly as it is. Sometimes you can almost hear the place give a sigh of relief when it feels this non-judgmental attention. It may soften or intensify and as you continue to be with it in a way that says, *"It's ok for you to be there, exactly the way you are now"*, it often opens up and starts to tell its story. As this unfolds, you can begin to understand the pain and listen in a more Compassionate way.

This total acceptance does not always bring immediate change to the place inside, but it does change *you*, because you are holding this part of yourself differently. Instead of feeling uptight about these horrible feelings inside – *"I shouldn't feel like this!"* – you relax and begin to feel okay about yourself for feeling all this. There is a deepening of kindness towards yourself, a healthy "self-love". This is a major step to becoming a whole person, welcoming home those parts of you that were split off or that you had been holding out on, judging and suppressing. And there's more - in doing this you begin to have a sense of who you truly are - that you are much larger than the wounded parts and can actually accept and embrace them. To have a real body feel of this is extremely freeing.

Letting go of our mind-sets of how we, others and the world should be and instead letting go into the reality of the present moment, is extremely powerful. It is also very much misunderstood. Accepting what is present and real now – inside and outside - is not the same as acquiescence. True acceptance does not turn you into a passive doormat for others. On the contrary, because of its non-reactive nature, it gives you the space inside to trust and allow intelligent and graceful resolution or action to arise that is fitting for the situation.

Presence and Identity

To be consistently present in this accepting way to what goes on inside creates a safe, inner climate in which deep change can happen. In Bio-Spiritual Focusing this bodily felt presence is called "caring feeling presence" and is specifically evoked and nourished as a way to develop inner kinship with what goes on inside. This is especially important when we are with painful feelings. As Gendlin said, *"Every 'bad' feeling is potential energy toward a more right way of being, if you give it the space to move toward its rightness"*. A gentle, caring presence creates a nurturing climate – Gendlin's space - so the feelings can move and change in the way only they know is right for them.

It is not always easy to maintain this sense of caring presence, especially when Focusing with intensely felt traumatized places, which may be overwhelming. But in the very struggle to find your own unique way to be present and caring, you are growing into your own sense of presence. For instance, you may need to find a place somewhere in the body that feels safe and unaffected, e.g. the sensation of your feet touching the ground can give a sense of safety and strength, a sense of your own presence that says *"I am here and all is well!"*

This is emphasized by Kevin McEvenue, an Alexander practitioner and Focusing trainer, in his teaching of "Wholebody Focusing". He places great importance on awareness of the body as a whole to provide a resource for being with difficult places. As Kevin says, *"When a part of me feels loved it awakens to its own healing"*.

As you continue to Focus you begin to increasingly experience that this sense of presence is who you truly are. A process is unfolding whereby you are gradually dis-identifying yourself from parts and places inside you with which you were previously identified. Your sense of identity is peeling away from entanglement with these parts. You begin to know yourself as that sense of presence: a simple sense of 'I Am-ness' that cannot be affected by anything that happens internally or externally. Nothing can be added and nothing can be taken away - I am simply present and aware.

Trusting A Larger Process

To practice letting go of the *"mind's omnipotent control"* of how Life, the Universe and Everything should be, encourages a humility to emerge in oneself. A deepening sense that *"I don't know and that's ok"*. A sense of being content with not knowing. Having Focused for quite a few years it has become clear to us that this humility brings a sensitivity and openness to a larger intelligence that is present within the physical body. An intelligence that can set in motion powerful healing processes. The body carries a wisdom, a knowing how to move things forward inside so that stuck or hurt places can be healed.

Focusing is all about allowing this *"broader wisdom within the entire human organism to speak"* . It is about getting sufficiently out of the way, by letting go of the mind's control, so that this body wisdom can express itself in its own unique way. So when we take our attention inside, it is clearly important that we have no investment in a specific result, but rather an openness and curious interest in where the body wisdom wants to take us.

But, our openness to the body's wisdom must be genuine. The body can't be fooled. It will know when there's still some kind of agenda, a wanting to fix and change things in a certain way. Our conditioning to assert our judgments as to what is good and bad and what should be and shouldn't be is deeply ingrained, so to let go to and trust this larger intelligence or process is a huge step along our spiritual path.

As we begin to allow the body wisdom to speak in and through ourselves, there's an undeniable sense that this wisdom or intelligence is much larger than we are. It's moving in us but is also carrying us in its unfolding.

Paradoxically, the body gives us the experience of being both whole in ourselves and yet, at the same time, part of something much larger. This may be experienced in different ways. For instance, it may feel like my feet are plugged into some large batteries hidden inside the ground and there's a strong sense of being connected with a flow of energy that is much larger than I am. Often in that flow there is a sense of Compassion for hurt places welling up which I could not feel on my own. I have a sense of being surrounded and supported by the whole earth, nature, the stars, the universe - a larger Presence or Process.

As Gendlin says:

> *"Your physically felt body is ...part of a gigantic system of here and other places, now and other times, you and other people - in fact, the whole universe. This sense of being bodily alive in a vast system is the body as it is felt from inside".*

Feeling part of a Larger Process is a natural spiritual need that is deeply etched in the psyche of human beings. It is often inadequately substituted by a sense of belonging to certain cults, groups or even religions. To have lost the experience of this *"sense of being bodily alive in a vast system"* has been the primary cause of much human misery.

Felt Shifts – "Grace Unfolding"

Once you have a felt sense of a place inside and it begins to open up, it will tell its story through a variety of symbols, such as images, words, insights or physical movement. As the story unfolds, something may begin to shift. Either the place itself or the way you are holding it may change.

Felt Shifts can sometimes happen in ways that could be described as "internal alchemy": the freeing up and transmutation of stagnant energy from stuck places inside us. This freed energy strengthens our sense of Presence. There's a sense of being more present, more vibrantly alive. In his book "The Power Of Now", Eckhart Tolle calls this *"internal alchemy or the transmutation of the base metal of suffering into the gold of consciousness"*.

These Felt Shifts are not of our own making. All we can do is to provide the right climate for these places to feel heard and to step back and wait to see what wants to happen. The body in all its wisdom inherently knows the direction in which these places need to move in order to be resolved, so that, ultimately, we can become whole.

When these shifts happen there is a sense of being gifted or 'graced' by the movement of a larger process at work through you. Like being in a river that powerfully flows towards its destination.

> *"Following the directions of Focusing is much like paddling a canoe from some protected inlet out into the middle of a river. Once there ....you soon discover that the stream has a life and movement on its own. It does not bend to your paddling any more than your canoe can change the course of the river's flow. All you can do is go with it in case it should catch you and carry you along."*

Peter Campbell and Ed McMahon.

Felt Shifts may be minute steps or they may be dramatic and instantly life changing. They may change the way you hold a certain issue or a certain situation in your life. They may open the door to creative solutions which your mind couldn't have thought of in its wildest dreams. Or they may unlock painful places. Whatever it brings, a Felt Shift always feels good inside. First, because we are at last beginning to know and accept ourselves; and second, because we are reconnecting with the movement of some Larger Process which deeply satisfies our spiritual need.

So Focusing facilitates this experience of the movement of the Larger Process through one's body and mind. To experience the immovability of one's own unique spirit, whilst also experiencing oneself being changed by the movement of a much Larger Process inside may seem paradoxical. But the world inside one's body is a different world, with paradox and contrasts happily living together.

Living In The Now

As Peter Campbell and Ed McMahon have said, there is a critical issue in our spiritual growth as human beings: the mind's *"omnipotent control"* . The thinking mind generates an incessant stream of thoughts. When we observe this seemingly unstoppable stream, it becomes obvious how much these thoughts take us out of the present moment, because most are related to either the past or the future.

The only access point to our own unique spirit and connection with a larger Process is the Here (our body) and Now (the present moment).

When Focusing becomes a way of living, you have a simple discipline that provides an excellent way of disengaging from the control of the thought stream and coming back home to the present moment. When you notice that you have jumped on a train of thought that has left the Here and Now, you can simply ask: *"How does it feel in my body to think these thoughts?"* This takes your attention inside your body and back to the present moment. This simple discipline, which can be done anytime, anywhere, offers us a way of living that keeps us connected to the dimension where we can be gifted by the intelligent energy of the larger Process.

Peacemaking From The Inside

As we begin to live this way, deep changes begin to happen in the way we relate to ourselves and others. Whenever something happens that triggers strong violent emotion, we are less likely to get swept away in the usual reactive cycle of violence-begetting-violence. Violent thoughts may be stirred up but by noticing them in a Focusing way you can unhook yourself from the violent thought stream and give yourself a choice in how to respond. This may not be easy in the heat of the moment and will take some practice, but even a few seconds of such bodily awareness can already be powerful. Even in such a short time there can be an experience of "grace", of something shifting in the way you are holding the situation.

When these feelings are 'graced' inside, it may also become clear whether there is some action to be taken with regard to the situation. You have broken the usual chain of reactive violence and any action you take now will come from a more peaceful way of being inside.

How to Use Focusing to Release Blocks to Action

Ann Weiser Cornell, PhD

Writer's block, procrastination, being a pack rat... all these are action blocks. If you want to start an exercise program but you don't, if you want to keep your desk clean but you don't, if you want to be more creative but it just doesn't happen, you are experiencing an action block--and Focusing can help.

Action blocks are painful, and everyone experiences them at times. For some people, the struggle dominates their lives. Are you familiar with wanting to do something day after day, even cursing and criticizing yourself for not doing it? Do you know about making resolution after resolution, even changing for a little while, but always sliding back? Wouldn't you love to be able to break that cycle and act easily and confidently instead?

Focusing releases the stuck system by changing the dynamic that holds the action block in place. In an action block, there is a part of you that isn't being heard. Ironically, that's the same part of you that seems to be in charge: the one that isn't taking action. It has you in its iron grip, and yet it's lonely, isolated, unacknowledged. No one has really asked it yet, "How come you're so set against taking action?" (Remember, being sure that you already know why is not the same thing as asking it!)

The Focusing process starts by bringing in self-Compassion instead of self-criticism. This alone begins the process of release, because self-criticism is the glue that holds the action block in place. It's funny, isn't it, that it often feels like just the opposite is true? I feel like my criticism of the part of me that won't exercise is my only hope of moving it, and that if I accept it, it will really take over my life! But actually, self-criticism holds the system in place because it ensures that the criticized part will not be heard, and everything will stay the same. And remember: Compassion and acceptance are not the same as agreement or giving in. I can still want to change, while being Compassionate to the part of me that doesn't want to.

Through Focusing, we create an inner atmosphere of safety, where any part of us can be heard without being attacked or criticized. This is important, because if you want to hear the truth and be released, you can't put pre-conditions on what you hear. "You can tell me anything except..." just won't work. In Focusing, it is quite literally true that the truth will set you free. So if you want to set the stage for allowing truth to come, start with an inner atmosphere of Compassion, if possible. (If something in you says "No" to being Compassionate, see if you can be Compassionate to that!)

Listening to the Part that Blocks You
Next, you call for the part of you that is blocking action to come forth and be known. You invite a felt sense of that part to come in your body. For example, when I was working on writer's block, the part of me that didn't want to write felt like a band across my chest. I didn't feel it most of the time, only if I sat down quietly in Focusing and deliberately asked my body to give me the feeling of not wanting to write. Then it came.

Next, acknowledge the felt sense and find a handle for it. Imagine you are sitting down with it to get to know it better, in a friendly, Compassionate way. Assume that it has some good reason for being the way it is--at least a good reason from its point of view.

One focuser, working on writer's block, sensed a rebellious adolescent part that didn't want to do what it was told. Another focuser, working on alcohol addiction, contacted a rageful demon that wanted to knock down cities. A focuser working on overeating found an emptiness in the stomach that asked for lots of patient attention.

These "parts that don't want to" all softened and changed with listening and attention. The miracle of Focusing is that sometimes Compassionate attention is all that's needed for any block to release. Often it not only releases, it also becomes part of the energy that moves you forward.

Listening to the Part that Wants to Change

The other Focusing technique that's helpful for releasing blocks to action is to listen to the part of you that wants to change. After you've spent time listening to the part that says, "I won't," be sure to also listen to the part that says, "I want to--and here's why." But don't let yourself get into the pain and struggle of not being able to do what you want to do. Instead, imagine that you are living a life in which this action is easy for you. See yourself at your desk writing, or in the gym exercising, or on stage, or in a new job, or whatever--beautifully, joyously, freely, and easily. Then ask your body to give you the felt sense that comes with that.

There is a positive forward movement contained in the part of you that wants to change. As long as it's in a struggle with the part that holds back, it's hard to feel the good energy that's there. But when you allow it to be felt, just as it would like to be, that good energy can come, and draw you forward.

Sometimes, of course, something else comes up when you are imagining the way you want to be. One focuser thought she wanted to be able to throw things away more easily. But when she focused on her house with nearly empty closets, she got a feeling of loss. That led her to some learning about why the block didn't want to release.

Either way you win: either you get the good energy and feel it draw you forward, or you discover something else that's in your way and needs your attention.

At the end of your session, be sure to make a commitment to a specific action at a specific time and place in the near future. Let it be something that both "sides" of you can agree to. Even if the action step you choose is small, it will make a big difference in your energy if you do something. Focusing alone isn't enough; the rest of you has to help out a little.

Getting released from action blocks and being able to act feels wonderful, and it's what more of us need if we're going to create the world we want. Thank goodness for Focusing!

This article appears in *The Radical Acceptance of Everything*, by Ann Weiser Cornell, PhD and featuring Barbara McGavin (Calluna Press; 2005).

Medical Decision Making

by Doralee Grindler Katonah, Psy.D., M.Div.
Presented at the 6th International Congress on Cancer,
Hong Kong University, Hong Kong, Nov. 1999.

I spoke with a man shortly after his wife of 45 years died. He was remembering a pivotal moment when his wife's illness began and she had been examined by several doctors. He recalled vividly the feeling of being in an office facing three doctors, all of whom were recommending exploratory colon surgery. Not only did they all agree about what they thought best but they were communicating a sense of urgency - we need to do this surgery immediately, before it is too late. He described how he felt the burden of making this decision and wanted desperately to do what would be best for his wife's health. He recalled looking over at her: "She just kept looking straight at me with this fear in her eyes about going through with the surgery." I saw the look but I didn't think it was important to explore this with her. I felt such time pressure and thought I should do what the doctors said. She had the surgery and they found nothing, but there were side-effects to the surgery that began her decline. He says to me: "I now look back and wished that I had allowed her to speak about her fear and to take the time to help her communicate to me what SHE sensed was best for her."

People diagnosed with cancer have to make very difficult decisions quickly. The physicians usually make a recommendation or present options along with the statistics. Often there is no clear-cut sense of what is best nor guarantees of a cure; while at the same time, they communicate the sense of urgency to decide. Often emotions are intense; patients and families are upset. And in this state, it is not easy to think through a decision, to weigh alternatives, to process the medical information productively. Yet, as Joan Borysenko points out: "The dominator model so prevalent in western medicine is no longer considered to be the most effective method of healing. People want more say in their treatment. Research already indicates that active participation in one's healing process does impact outcome."

There are several typical ways in which people tend to approach this decision-making task. Many people go into their heads and try to weigh the logic presented by the doctors to make their decision. Sometimes decisions are made by family members who have a strong opinion about what is best and push for it. This family pressure often silences and disempowers the patient. Others just assume "the doctor knows best" and abdicate a more active involvement in decisions.

If decisions are made in any of these ways there is a certain way in which the person of the patient has stepped aside and is not involved.

If we recall the woman with the look of fear in her eyes. In a sense that look has something to say too. There is a "you" deep down inside - the inner you that is your aliveness behind everything that is also responding to what is happening and has a perspective that needs to be included. Our life experiences create in us sensitivities and dispositions and skills of thinking which can be accessed by attending to a felt sense in your body. This is different than emotions and different than just thinking about the decision. The felt sense is concretely felt but at first without words. If attended to, it begins to speak and offers a perspective or an action step that you could not access through a logical approach. This information when taken into consideration brings with it a sense of centeredness that is felt in the body. This is a kind of bodily wisdom that supports parasympathetic activity and wisely guides you towards healing.

This process can have a powerful function in the process of medical decision-making. I will now present two case vignettes to illustrate how this works. The first case demonstrates the use of focusing to find an inner step that will help the person make a crucial decision regarding her treatment for breast cancer. In the second case, I will follow a person over time while making several decisions and how attending to her felt sense helped her in this process.

Carol is a woman in her 40's who had just been diagnosed with breast cancer. She had received both a first and second opinion from two topnotch physicians. Her father who also was an oncologist agreed with their recommendations. All three doctors were aggressively recommending a program of treatments including an initial surgery, a follow-up surgery, and chemotherapy. When she contacted her therapist she was breathless with anxiety and a sense of urgency. As she began to speak she spoke rapidly and her words were filled with "they said...." Then they said I have to...." If we just look at the language itself, the repeated use of the word "they", expresses how she was filled up with the physicians' perspective. There was no space inside her yet for her to even begin to sense her own responses to the diagnosis and the recommendations. This began a focusing session.

THERAPIST: I want to say to you that you can take the time, right now, to come down inside yourself and see where YOU are with all of this. What feels right to you? "What is YOUR sense of what you need right now?"

PWC: (SILENCE) Oh, what comes there is, I want to see the X rays. My father used to take me to the hospital with him when I was a child. He showed me how to read x-rays. That is what comes now. I want to see for myself what they are talking about. Oh, I guess I could ask the surgeon to show me.

(When a step comes from the body like this, it is important to resonate it back to the body to see if this is right.)

THERAPIST: Notice what came there and check and see if your body resonates with that. Ask yourself; is this what I need to do next?

PWC: (Silent attention to her body) Yes, I feel a sense of release now in my body. It's like a breath of fresh air.

(This feedback from the body usually takes the form of a feeling of release or increase in energy which further confirms the message that came.)

Notice how specific the perspective is that came there. "I want to see the x-rays. " It is very individual to her and based upon a significant childhood experience. No therapist or health care professional could ever have come up with this for her. And this particular step will not fit for other patients. It is only her body that knows what is uniquely needed in order to come to a decision that feels right to her.

THERAPIST: You are going to be pressured to move very fast. You need to continue to make a space to sense from your body WHAT IS RIGHT FOR YOU.

(This inner step that came which she followed through on led her to decide to go with the doctors' recommendations but with a different feel inside herself. She no longer felt so frantic and scared.)

PWC: I know I have many hurdles in front of me, but I sort of feel like I have a place in myself to stand.

This second vignette follows a cancer patient over time through several decisions. She is a long-term cancer survivor as it is now 11 years since her diagnosis. of breast cancer. She also knew focusing quite well before her diagnosis so she was able to rely upon listening to her felt senses relatively easily. Still there was a time when she really didn't know what was right. Later she made a decision that went against medical advice.

Reva is a 66 year-old woman, married, with four adult children and 6 grandchildren. Her cancer was discovered as a result of a routine mammogram. After the mammogram came back positive her gynecologist referred her to a surgeon.

She went to her appointment alone. Reva describes herself as a very independent person so it didn't occur to her to ask anyone to come with her. She was waiting in the doctor's office. Now when someone is facing this kind of crisis, sometimes they feel the urge to act differently, to allow a new part of themselves to grow. As Reva awaited her first consultation with this surgeon she did something different. In her words now:

REVA: Then a person I know walked by and saw me sitting there and said, "Hi!. How are you doing and what are you doing here?" And I told her what I was doing and she said, "Would you like me to wait with you?" I'm a very independent person and generally I do everything myself, but I remember saying to her, "You know, I really would." That was probably one of my first big steps toward my healing - because I did something different. I even asked her to go in to see the doctor with me because I was worried whether I would actually hear everything she had to say.

Reva noticed her bodily response towards her friend's invitation. This enabled her to respond differently than she would have in the past which enabled her to have more support during this crucial visit. The first physician was also authoritarian in her manner and didn't discuss options but rather insisted that a mastectomy was the only answer.

REVA: The woman surgeon turned out to be very unexpectedly hard - straightforward - kind of unfeeling. To have my "friend" there with me really made a difference. With her support I was able to pay attention to how this interview felt in my body, I decided to seek a second opinion.

After this appointment Reva went to the library and picked several books on cancer to read. This is when she learned about a lumpectomy. The second doctor had a more collaborative style and also thought that a lumpectomy could be performed. Reva didn't want to choose a doctor and decide about treatment until she found a sense of rightness in her body. She noticed that the second doctor was warm and caring and considered options with her. She described noticing that after meeting with him she felt confident. She decided to work with him and went through the surgery.

Because there was lymph node involvement, her doctor thought that she should have chemotherapy. Her oncologist recommended that she participate in a research program and receive the treatment that was randomly assigned to her. He insisted that he didn't know which treatment would be better; that is why they are doing the study. This was a very difficult decision for Reva to make, especially because the doctor kept telling her that he didn't know what was best She turned to her support community.

REVA: My friends just held me and I cried in a way I never had before. I felt so little. After a while the sobbing stopped and I felt renewed and more of my strength came back. I then decided to sit with the sense in my body about the decision I was about to make. What came was: "I don't know enough. The doctor doesn't know. Just go with the research and trust."

She received the highest dosage treatment. The side-effects were debilitating. She was sick, she lost her hair. But slowly her body recovered and her hair began to grow back. Then Spring came and she was scheduled for another round of chemotherapy as defined by the research protocol. Again she focused and she began to notice a sense of uneasiness within.

REVA: This time, there was something about it that just didn't feel right.

THERAPIST: Can you just give your attention to that sense of "not feeling right."

R: (Silence) I got this very clear message, "You don't need any more chemotherapy and if you take it you're abusing your body. You're doing harm to yourself because the stuff is so strong and it just wipes out so much." The message was: "You don't need any more."

(Notice how specific and certain this inner message is. It really can happen like this, but the next question is what do you do with this kind of message from your body)

Reva now describes what happened after this focusing session.

REVA: I immediately went to the phone and called some good friends I could talk to about this. I couldn't get anyone. Nobody was available and I had to go to the doctor's. Once I was at the doctor's the message came again, "You don't need anymore." And it was scary. I didn't know whether or not to go with this inner message.

REVA: But I went to the doctor and I told him. He was very upset with me. He told me my results couldn't be used - that I was messing up the protocol and they really needed this data. I kept saying: "I know that I have to do this...this is what's good for me. I'm sorry about all of that and I have to say NO."

Reva followed the messages she received from her bodily felt sense several times. Once the message she got went against what the doctor was recommending. This was an important juncture for her, to choose to trust this message and Reva continued to recover successfully from her cancer. She looks back upon her cancer journey:

R: I found within myself a strength I didn't know I had. I learned how to ask for help. I found out that I wasn't alone as I had always felt myself to be. I found an inner strength that I continue to rely upon.

Reva has been free of cancer for 12 years.

Here are two different examples of ways to apply focusing to the decision-making process. I want to summarize with four simple points.

1. It is important to be informed about the illness and the treatment options. This provides the field from which the person can sense inside for their own inner sense of what is needed or right for them. So, people need to be encouraged to ask questions and seek more information so that their felt sense is fully informed. The patient could be told: "Take a little time now to sit with what I have said and ask the questions that emerge." "Are there any other concerns that you have."

2. The Felt SENSE is not the same as the intense emotion; however, intense emotions may need to be expressed because if they remain unexpressed, they may block one from accessing the questions that are there and the action steps that will help one find a centered place re. their decision.
3. Communicate to people that they have the time to sense inside for what they need to make a decision that "feels" right in their body. Physicians could say: "It is important that this be your decision and that you come to a sense of confidence and inner assuredness about the direction to proceed. There may be other steps you need to take to help you come to your decision. Take the time you need to come to this resolution."
4. In honoring this form of knowing you are helping the person with cancer find a centeredness and an inner consent to treatment or an alternative to treatment. This is bringing mind/body and spirit together for the sake of healing.

Sondra Perl's Composing Guidelines

Sandra Perl, Ph.D.

These writing guidelines will help you discover more of what is on your mind and almost on your mind. If they seem artificial, think of them as "exercises." But they are exercises that will help you to perform certain subtle but crucial mental operations that most skilled and experienced writers do naturally:

- Continue writing, even when you don't know where you're going.

- Periodically pause and ask, "What's this all about?"

- Periodically check what you have written against your internal sense of where you're going or what you wanted to say--your "felt sense."

Your teacher may guide you through the Perl guidelines in class. If it feels too mechanical to follow them in a group setting, remember that the goal is to teach you a procedure you can use on your own. But we can teach it best by giving you a taste of it in practice--which means trying it out in class. It's hard to learn the guidelines alone because your old writing habits are so strong.

After some practice with each of the directives or questions that follow, you'll be able to sense how to distribute your time yourself.

1. Find a way to get comfortable. Shake out your hands, take a deep breath, settle into your chair. Close your eyes if you'd like to; relax. Find a way to be quietly and comfortably aware of your inner state.

2. Ask yourself, "What's going on with me right now? Is there anything in the way of my writing today?" When you hear yourself answering, take a minute to jot down a list of any distractions or impediments that come to mind.

3. Now ask yourself, "What's on my mind? Of all the things I know about, what might I like to write about now?" When you hear yourself answering, jot down what comes. Maybe you get one thing, maybe a list. If you feel totally blocked, you may write down "Nothing." Even this can be taken further by asking yourself, "What is this `Nothing' all about?"

4. Ask yourself, "Now that I have a list--long or short--is there anything else I've left out, any other piece I'm overlooking, maybe even a word I like, something else I might want to write about sometime that I can add to this list?" Add anything that comes to mind.

5. Whether you have one definite idea or a whole list of things, look over what you have and ask, "What here draws my attention right now? What could I begin to write about, even if I'm not certain where it will lead?" Take the idea, word, or item and put it at the top of a new page. (Save the first page for another time.)

6. Now--taking a deep breath and settling comfortably into your chair-- ask yourself, "What are all the associations and parts I know about this topic? What can I say about it now?" Spend as long as you need writing down these responses. Perhaps it will be a sustained piece of freewriting or stream of consciousness, or perhaps separate bits, a long list, or notes to yourself.

7. Now having written for a while, interrupt yourself, set aside all the writing you've done, and take a fresh look at this topic or issue. Grab hold of the *whole* topic--not the bits and pieces--and ask yourself, "What makes this topic interesting to me? What's *important* about this that I haven't said yet? What's the *heart* of this issue?" Wait quietly for a *word, image,* or *phrase* to arise from your "felt sense" of the topic. Write whatever comes. (For more on "felt sense," see "Ruminations and Theory" at the end of this unit.)

8. Take this word or image and use it. Ask yourself, "What's this all about? Describe the feeling, image, or word. As you write, let the "felt sense" deepen. Where do you feel that "felt sense"? In your head, stomach, forearms? Where in your body does it seem centered? Continue to ask yourself, "Is this right? Am I getting closer? Am I saying it?" See if you can feel when you're on the right track. See if you can feel the shift or click inside when you get close, "Oh yes, this says it."

9. If you're at a dead end, you can ask yourself, "What makes this topic so hard for me?" or "What's so difficult about this?" Again pause and see if a word, image, or phrase comes to you that captures this difficulty in a fresh way--and if it will lead you to some more writing.

10. When you find yourself stopping, ask, "What's missing? what hasn't yet gotten down on paper?" and again look to your "felt sense" for a *word or* an image. Write what comes to mind.

11. When again you find yourself stopping, ask yourself, "Where is this leading? What's the point I'm trying to make?" Again write down whatever comes to mind.

12. Once you feel you're near or at the end, ask yourself, "Does this feel complete?" Look to your "felt sense," your gut reaction, even to your body, for the answer. Again write down whatever answer comes to you. If the answer is "No," pause and ask yourself, "What's missing?" and continue writing.

About the Perl Guidelines

These guidelines sometimes work differently for different people--and even differently for you on different occasions. The main thing to remember is that they are meant for you to use on your own, flexibly, in your own way. There is nothing sacred about the exact format or wording. They are not meant to be a straitjacket. To help you in adapting them to your own needs, here is a list of what are probably the four pivotal moments:

•   Relax, stretch, clear your mind, try to attend quietly to what's inside-- and note any distractions or feelings that may be preventing you from writing.

•   Start with a list of things you could write about. Often we can't find what we really want to write about till the third or fourth item--or not till that subtle after--question, "Is there something else I might have forgotten?"

- As you are writing, periodically pause and look to that felt sense somewhere inside you--that feeling, image, or word that somehow represents what you are trying to get at--and ask whether your writing is really getting at it. This comparing or checking back ("Is this it?") will often lead to a productive "shift" in your mind ("Oh *now* I see what it is I want to say").

- Finally, toward the end, ask, "What's this all about? Where does this writing seem to be trying to go?" And especially ask, "What's missing? What *haven't* I written about?"

The specific details of the procedure are much less important than the charitable, supportive, and generative spirit behind the whole thing.

On Felt Sense

Felt sense may seem a vague concept, but we get new leverage in our writing if we realize that there is always *something* there "in mind" before we have words for it. In one sense, of course, we *don't* know something till we have it in words. But in another sense we do indeed know quite a lot, and it's a question of learning to tap it better.

So what is it that's in mind before we find words? Is it some set of words that's farther inside our heads-fainter or in smaller print? If so, what lies behind *them* to guide or produce them? Behind our words, then, inevitably, some nonverbal feeling or "sense."

You can easily prove this mysterious phenomenon to yourself by asking yourself after you've been writing a while, the crucial question: "Is this what I've been wanting to say?" What's interesting is that we can almost always give an answer. Then we need to ask this: "What is the basis for our answer--for our being able to say, 'Yes, this really is what I was wanting to say,' or 'No, that's not it,' or 'Sort of, but not quite'?" We haven't got *words* for what's in mind, but we have *something against* which we can match the words we've used to see whether they are adequate to our intention. We know what we want to say well enough to realize that we have or haven't said it.

"Felt sense" is what Eugene Gendlin has named this internal awareness that we call on. And his point--which we too want to emphasize--is that we can learn to call on it better. (It may seem odd or unfashionable to suggest that our felt sense of what we're writing about might be located in a part the body. But many people experience what's "in mind" not just "in the head" but also--as they say-- in the "gut.")

The crucial operation in the Perl process is when you pause and *attend* to that felt sense--pause and say, "What's my *feeling* for what I'm getting at" (or "What's my image or word?"). You *then* ask yourself, "Have I said it?" The most productive situation, ironically, is when you answer, "No." For in that moment of experiencing a mismatch or *non*fit between your words and your felt sense, *you tend to experience a click or shift that moves you closer to knowing this thing that you can't yet say.* In short, pausing, checking, and saying "No" usually lead you to better words.

One reason people don't pause and check their words against their felt sense often enough is that they get too discouraged at the negative answer. They think that the question is a *test* and that the negative answer means they've failed the test. *("Again* I've proved that I'm no good at finding words!") They don't realize that if you ask the question of yourself in the right way--in a charitable and constructive spirit--"No" is the better answer: it can always lead you to a better understanding of what you are trying to get at.

Remember, however, that when we urge you to attend more to your felt sense and then pause and check your words against it, we're *not* saying that thing that perhaps you've heard too often: "Stop! What is your *thesis?"* It's not, "What is your thesis?" but rather "What is the physical feeling or image you have that somehow *stands for* what you're wanting to say?" You haven't *got* a thesis yet-- haven't got the right words yet--but you do have a genuinely available feeling for what you're trying to get at. If you check any trial set of words against that feeling, you can tell whether or not they are what you were trying to say.

Three Rules for Safety in Focusing Partnerships

Ann Weiser Cornell

"Adapted from an article by Ann Weiser Cornell appearing in *The Focusing Connection* newsletter, January 2000."

1. Never never never mention the content of the Focusing session, even after the session is over, unless the Focuser brings it up.

This is really important. Many a Focusing partnership has broken up on the rocks of this one. A seemingly innocent, well-intentioned comment can compromise the safety of the partnership for both people. And it's so tempting to do it! You have to be really clear, and really conscious, on this one, because the easiest thing out of your mouth is probably something that will violate this rule. We have thousands of times more practice being social in a non-Focusing setting than in a Focusing one. What could it hurt? Answer: a lot.

Let's say your partner is Focusing on feelings around an argument with their spouse. During the session you scrupulously follow the guidelines, and just reflect their feelings and their point of view, without putting in any opinions of your own. But after the session is over, when the two of you are still sitting there, or standing up to go, or in the kitchen sharing a cup of tea, you find yourself saying, X [the spouse] is really a difficult person. What happens? The next time your partner wants to focus on that issue or a similar one, there is a tilt, a slant. A part of them thinks it can win you to its side. Another part feels unsafe, like you have taken sides against it. You have shown your *bias*, and bias creates an unsafe space.

It's even worse if your casual comment implies some judgement or criticism of the Focuser, like: I would never put up with the kinds of thing you put up with from X. Now the bias includes a judgement of the Focuser, and the space is even less safe for Focusing.

Worst of all: advice of any kind. Giving advice unasked-for implies both judgement and lack of trust. Think about it! When you say Why don't you try... or "Have you thought about..." or "What I would do if I were you is...", you're actually saying that you don't believe they can handle this situation wisely without your input. Is that what you actually believe? You may want to Focus on that with another partner!

It's another matter if advice is *asked for*. "What do you think?" or "What would you do?" are clear invitations to give your opinion. The problem I think for many people (and I'm not just talking about Focusing partnerships now) is that they hear the statement of a problem *as if* it were a request for advice. Y was talking about her painful wrist during a Focusing session and her listener Z, after the session was over, started asking, "Have you tried orthobionomy? I can give you the name of a really good practitioner." There is no doubt that Z had the very best of intentions. But the loss of safety from the intrusion was a greater cost than the possible gain from the good advice. Y has plenty of people to give her advice, but only a few Focusing partners.

No matter how you met your partner, whether they were a friend to start with, or someone you met in a workshop, this close relationship will start to feel like a friendship. And then there can be a clash between the rules and mores of friendship, and the stricter ones of Focusing partnership. It might be good to recognize the potential for conflict within yourself, the part of you that wants the ease and flow of a regular friendship, the part of you that wants the safety of a Focusing partnership. Friends express opinions, friends give advice (although probably a lot more than they need to!), friends share stories of similar experiences. You have to ask yourself, is the feeling of relaxed unstructured friendship with this person really worth the risk to the Focusing partnership? I'd say no, don't risk it. A good Focusing partner is not that easy to find!

"What do I do if my partner mentions the content of my session and I'm uncomfortable with that?"

If you catch it at the moment it happens, you might say something like, "It feels like you're talking about the content of my session, and I know you mean well, but I'd like to leave some space around that." Or "....but I'd like to leave that whole topic alone now."

148

If, as often happens, you only realize later that you were uncomfortable with your partner commenting on your content, that's a trickier situation. You might ask yourself, in a Focusing way, if your sense of safety with your partner needs for you to bring up the subject of what has already happened. If not, you could just resolve to catch it if it happens again. But if you do need to bring it up, you might say, "Do you remember last time when we were chatting after the session, and you said, "I would never put up with the kinds of thing you put up with from X."? I realized later that it felt like you were commenting on the content of my session, and I'd like to make a request that we not comment on the content of one another's session unless the Focuser brings it up. Would that be OK?" There are two key points here (with appreciation to Marshall Rosenberg's Non-Violent Communication, even though I'm not following his system exactly). One is to quote, to the best of your ability, exactly what your partner said, as opposed to something like: "Do you remember last time when we were chatting after the session, and you criticized my relationship?" Two is to remember that your partner was well-intentioned and this is not to judge their behavior as wrong, but just to let them know that you would like something different in the future.

"What if the Listener gets triggered by the Focuser's material?"

First answer: Good! What a great opportunity!

Second answer: As the Listener, you are responsible for your own feelings and reactions, of course. You are a real person, not impervious to being moved or touched or shaken or stirred by what the Focuser is working on. But they are *yours*. I'd recommend saying "Hello, I know you're there," silently, to any feelings of your own that come up while you're listening to the Focuser. That may be enough. There is no need to share them. In fact, better not, not even after the session is over. They're too likely to infringe on your partner's content.

If your turn is next, there may be a way to sensitively Focus on your issues that were triggered by your partner's work. If you can really own them as yours, not in any way "about" your partner, it should be OK. If you're in doubt, you can check with your partner by briefly describing what you want to work on and asking if that would or wouldn't violate their space. This sort of mutually inspired work can actually be rewarding for both people.

The most dangerous type of "being triggered" is when you don't realize it, so that instead of you taking responsibility for your reactions, they emerge as criticisms, judgments (of the Focuser or others in the Focuser's life), advice, or rescuing behavior. Earlier, I said that giving advice is probably out of social habit or because you mistakenly believe you've been asked for help. Actually, the urge to give advice, rescue, help, or judge may well be coming from a place in you that is having a hard time just being with the Focuser's process. *Be alert for the urge to help, fix, or rescue.* These urges can be golden signposts that there is something in you that needs some company.

2. Remember that it is the Focuser's session, and it is not your responsibility as Listener/Guide/Companion/Ally to make something good happen in their Focusing, or even to make sure they're Focusing at all.

This used to happen quite frequently: We would finish the Level One Focusing class, and the people would go forth to practice with each other as partners. Then I would start getting the phone calls: "I'm not sure that my partner is really Focusing. What can I do about it?"

My answer: "Nothing. There is nothing you can or should do about it. The Focusing is your partner's responsibility. You're there to listen, hold the space, be present. That's all."

I got tired of the phone calls, so I got smart, and now I teach this in the course. The locus of responsibility between Focusing partners is this: when someone is Focusing, it's their session. It's their time. Period. If they want to use it to talk about instead of sense into, that's their business. If they want to use it to brainstorm or set goals or meditate, that's their business. Just ask how they would like you to be with them. Then you don't have to worry about your role.

"I get bored when my partner tells long stories about other people. I keep waiting for them to get a felt sense."

Here we have a paradox. On the one hand, we teach you that what really brings change is to do Focusing: to bring interested awareness to a felt sense. On the other hand, we say, it's the Focuser's session, whatever they want to do, just be with that. How to resolve this? How about this: what if you really knew, what if you really *trusted*, that your partner's stories are part of a holistic process? Would you still be bored? Or would you, perhaps, sit back and watch curiously, interested to see where and how that process would unfold?

There is one legitimate way to influence your partner's Focusing, and that is, when it's your turn, do great Focusing yourself. If they really aren't getting satisfaction from whatever they're doing, and they see how much you're getting from Focusing, they'll change. In their own time, in their own way.

3. Divide your time together into equal turns.

I had a lovely and precious Focusing partnership that lasted, weekly, for fourteen years. For approximately the first eleven years of that time, I would drive up to my partner's house, switch off my car's ignition, and think, "Too bad nothing's going to come up for me tonight." Week after week, without fail, that same thought would come, even though week after week, without fail, I had Focusing sessions in which something *did* come and unfolded and brought insight and relief. (Even though you can trust the Focusing process, you cannot necessarily trust your thoughts about it before it starts!)

If my partner and I had not had the rule, "Divide your time together into equal turns," I might have been tempted to say to her, "I don't need to Focus tonight, why don't you take all the time." And that would have been, as I hope you can feel, profoundly undermining to the partnership relationship. It also would have been a shame, because I would have missed all those great sessions.

People are different. Some have a lot going on, a lot of the time. We call that (as I learned from my first Focusing teachers, Elfie Hinterkopf and Les Brunswick), "Close Process." Some people, like me, usually think that nothing will come. That's called "Distant Process." Both kinds of people can and do get a lot out of Focusing. They can even get a lot out of being partners for each other. But the Distant Person should not, repeat *not*, be tempted to give away their time to the Close Person because the Close Person seems to need it more. They don't. Everyone needs Focusing. (Besides, a person who is upset or going through a tough time can get a lot out of being the Listener, a feeling of centeredness, the self-esteem of being able to be there for someone else....)

"Equal turns" can be equal in time, or simply equal in opportunity. For example, if two people make an agreement that they will each Focus as long as they want to, that's equal, even if one session is forty minutes and the other ten. Also, the turns don't have to be at the same time: some partnerships have a deal where one week is one person's turn, and the next week is the other person's turn. That's OK. It's even OK if one of you always wants to go first and the other one always wants to go second. The only thing that's not OK is not taking your turn, because that alters the power relationship of the partnership, and marks one person as "needier" and the other as "the giver." Giving away your turn is not a trusting thing to do, neither trusting in the other, nor in your own process. Trust, and take your turn.

On the other side of the coin, if you happen to be the partner with the Close Process, be scrupulous about finding a comfortable stopping place for your

151

session when the agreed ending time has come. If you're full of feelings, of course there will be a temptation to go over, especially if you're enjoying the space your partner gives you. Don't. It's a dangerous indulgence, because, maybe not the first time, and maybe not the second time, but if this happens too often, then you will have become the "needy one" and I guarantee you won't like how that feels. Unless you are really sure that the other person feels relaxed about time, as you do, better to respect time boundaries as agreed. It's part of the "care and feeding" of a Focusing partner.

Of course we are not machines and it should always be possible to renegotiate time agreements if needed. If I give a two minute warning and my partner says, "It feels like this needs five more minutes, is that OK?" I feel much better about being asked, like that, than if my partner goes over time without asking. I also feel better if such a thing is asked for only rarely, as a special request, rather than regularly. Others may feel differently. The key is to respect your partner's needs, and your own.

.

Focusing Steps: Short Form

Developed by Gene Gendlin, Ph.D.
Modified by Lucinda Gray, Ph.D.

1--Clearing a Space, **taking an inventory of what's up with you right now, what might be between you and feeling really great right now.** Pose a question inside, then check in your body for a response to this question. There are many ways the question can be framed, find one that works for you.

When a feeling comes up, spend a few moments with it, name it and acknowledge it, then gently make a space for it to be put aside for right now. You may have to promise it you'll work on it later; so that you can now go on to find out what else might be there. Do several rounds, checking in your body to see if the feeling has been moved aside. Eventually you will reach a clear open spacious feeling in your body even though you now have a stack of issues to look at. Spend a few moments enjoying the clear space inside.

2--Felt Sensing, **pick which one is number 1, or which one you want to work on. Or maybe it picks you. Take time with sensing underneath the feeling or sensation for the "more of it", Stay with the feeling so that you can begin to touch into that still unclear edge of the "all" of it, the whole of what's there.** All about how you're carrying it in your body right now. It's important here to take plenty of time and slow down so that the Felt Sense can form from the fuzzy unclear "more" that's there.

3--Getting a handle, staying in your body and allowing a word, phrase, image or gesture—to emerge from the Felt Sense. Let whatever comes to just drift through your awareness until something comes that really seems to fit, or "click" with your body sense. Wait patiently for the right symbol to emerge.

4--Resonating, stay with the new symbol that came and go back and forth from your Felt Sense to the words or image, checking how they connect. If it is the right symbol, word, or image there will be some body reaction to it, your body will somehow let you know; the feeling will become more intense, or there will be a loosening, the beginning of a release inside.

5--Asking, as you stay with the body feeling, ask a question of the feeling, a question that might help the feeling open into some new form; For example- what's the worst part, hardest part of all this? Or, what needs to happen for this to be all OK with me? Or, what would it feel like if somehow this was all fixed?

6--Receiving—The Felt Shift, see if there is some change in your body. If something new comes, stay with this new knowing that is coming. The Felt Shift happens when your body recognizes the whole truth, the rightness of the symbolization that has come, and something changes inside. There is a feeling of release and relief. Take time to enjoy the feeling of letting go, and check the new information with your body sense a few times to mark the place, so that you will recognize this as a starting point next time. You may want to make a few notes.

Focusing: Short Form

Eugene Gendlin, Ph.D.

1. Clear a space

How are you? What's between you and feeling fine?
Don't answer; let what comes in your body do the answering.
Don't go into anything.
Greet each concern that comes. Put each aside for a while, next to you.
Except for that, are you fine?

2. Felt Sense

Pick one problem to focus on.
Don't go into the problem.
What do you sense in your body when you sense the whole of that problem?
Sense all of that, the sense of the whole thing, the murky discomfort or the
unclear body-sense of it.

3. Get a handle

What is the quality of the felt sense?
What one word, phrase, or image comes out of this felt sense?
What quality-word would fit it best?

4. Resonate

Go back and forth between word (or image) and the felt sense.
Is that right?
If they match, have the sensation of matching several times.
If the felt sense changes, follow it with your attention.
When you get a perfect match, the words (images) being just right for this feeling, let yourself feel that for a minute.

5. Ask

"What is it, about the whole problem, that makes me so _____?
When stuck, ask questions:
What is the worst of this feeling?
What's really so bad about this?
What does it need?
What should happen?
Don't answer; wait for the feeling to stir and give you an answer.
What would it feel like if it was all OK?
Let the body answer
What is in the way of that?

6. Receive

Welcome what came. Be glad it spoke.
It is only one step on this problem, not the last.
Now that you know where it is, you can leave it and come back to it later.
Protect it from critical voices that interrupt.
Does your body want another round of focusing, or is this a good stopping place?

FOCUSING

LEARN FROM THE MASTERS

TRAINING MANUAL IV

Focusing in Education

Lucinda Gray, Ph.D.

Focusing is already being applied in many different settings and is being taught in graduate schools all over the world. There is extensive work being done teaching Focusing to children at all educational levels, although most of the research has been done with younger children, and with college students rather than with adolescents.

In approaching a school system where Focusing is new, we recommend beginning with teaching the teachers and the administrative staff rather than starting directly with the students. Unless the staff is receptive and understands the principals of Focusing students won't be able to benefit and use their Focusing skills at school.

Focusing has been the subject of massive effectiveness research. Studies show that the first stage of the Focusing process, Clearing a Space, is an effective tool in increasing performance of complex mental tasks, one example of which is arithmetic (Zimring, 1974, 1983, 1985, 1990). It increases capacity to attend to problems, and improves school behavior. Clearing a Space has also been studied as a therapeutic method in increasing self-care, self-esteem and sense of wellbeing in cancer patients, trauma victims, and overweight persons attempting to lose weight, among other studies.

Learning Focusing is always a voluntary process. It cannot work when it is required. Therefore in starting this project we convinced the principal that mastery of the Focusing process not be a requirement. Therefore teachers in this program were required to attend the trainings, but not required to "learn" the process or practice it on their own.

Although research is not the primary purpose of teaching Focusing in schools, we suggest teachers be asked for their reactions to the training and their feedback on how it works for them personally at home and at school. The purpose of this qualitative research is to further our knowledge of how Focusing can be applied in other educational settings, and its effectiveness.

In the school setting Focusing can be applied for calming and centering and letting go of distractions that get in the way of teaching and learning. It can also be used to help students work with blocks to motivation, to increase frustration tolerance and emotional resilience. Specifically students can find action steps that will help them move toward a life path that fits for them, and release inner resistance to advancement.

Focusing teaches a very specific nonjudgmental way of listening that can radically change interaction patterns in the classroom between teachers and students. By listening to what is happening for the student in the more receptive way taught in Focusing, problems are often quickly resolved. Teachers find that by taking a few moments to listen to the students experience they actually save time and energy. Students are more open to disclosing problems that may be slowing down their learning process. With open disclosure of feelings, solutions are more rapidly arrived at and less time is spent on classroom discipline. For students, blocks to attention dissolve more quickly so that the whole teaching process becomes more efficient.

The earlier a child learns Focusing the better, because the child benefits in every way, educationally, emotionally and in physical health. We believe that adolescents have a great need for Focusing because they face a major life transition in separating from families and becoming self-supporting members of our society. We believe that high school is a crucial stage of development that is of central importance to the development of young adults.

How Focusing Can Contribute to Resilience Training in Schools

Diana Marder, Ph.D.

Something different was happening at North Junior High in St. Cloud, Minnesota. Between school years 1997-98 and 1998-99, suspensions were 70% lower; fights were reduced by 63.8%, and incidents of violence dropped 65.1%. Staff made comments such as "The kids are respectful...our mood is lighter...we are having such a nice year".

These changes were the result of several years of training of faculty, staff, and students in Resilience/Health Realization programs developed by the National Resilience Resource Center. "Health Realization is a principle-based understanding of how human beings function." Its basic principles are

a. "We create our experience of life with our thinking...we create our personal reality with our thinking.

b. Every person has wisdom within. At the very core, every person is whole... The healthy self is never destroyed and it can always be realized. Health realization.... builds confidence in trusting the unknown, waiting and noticing fresh insights, out-of-the blue 'ahas'."

c. Humans are "more than our thinking, feelings, and behaviors. We are the 'observer' who [recognizes] our thinking...You are the noticer".

In developing these principles, the Center staff was "looking for strategies that would increase the '*health of the helper*'". Earlier resilience research focused on the study of people who had overcome significant stress and trauma, and looked for what was unique in their lives and personalities. More recent research, however, has focused on what qualities of *systems* promote resilience in *all* members of the system. Three main factors have been identified:

1. "Caring and supportive relationships that provide support, Compassion, and trust;

2. Encouraging high expectations that convey respect and build on the strengths of each person; and

3. Opportunities for participation and contribution that provide real responsibilities...a sense of ownership and belonging, and ultimately, a sense of spiritual connectedness and meaning." [1]

Kathy Marshall points out, however, that the research which identified factors 1-3, does not tell us how to teach *adults* to become the kind of people that could provide caring and supportive relationships to the youth they work with.

In *Reculturing Systems with Resilience/Health Realization*,[2] Kathy Marshall points out that in order for school staffs to provide the kind of atmosphere that fosters resilience, they must themselves believe in human potential-- that every individual has the capacity for health and well-being. School systems, too, can be viewed in terms of whether youth are seen as at-risk or "at-promise". If adult staff discover their own perhaps-buried capacity for positive growth, they are much more apt to believe in the (also perhaps hidden) growth potential of their students. Principles a and c above spell out these beliefs in more detail.

Can Focusing contribute to a school environment which promotes the health of the helper and fosters resilience in all its students? We of the Focusing community believe that it can, because the core principles and practices of Focusing are intimately connected to the principles of health realization.

Principles a and b are, in fact, at the core of Focusing.
Focusing was born out of Eugene Gendlin's work as a colleague of world-

---

[1] Bonnie Bernard, 1991, cited in Marshall, Kathy, *National Resilience Resource Center, Bridging the Gap in* Waxman, H., Padron, Y., and Gray,J. *Educational Resiliency. p. 6*

[2]*http://www.cce.umn.edu/pdfs/NRRC/resil_health_realization.pdf*

renowned psychologist Carl Rogers, who developed the idea of the actualizing tendency. The human organism, he believes, has an inborn tendency to grow toward greater health. What prevents and distorts this growth is the fact that our need for approval may be even stronger than our need for growth. When we are raised with *conditions of worth,* we lose conscious access to parts of our experience, and without this access, are hampered in our growth. Given sufficient time in an environment of empathy, positive regard, and congruence, the growth tendency is restored. To this, Gendlin added his philosophical belief that development comes from an interaction of experiencing and *symbolizing.*

Gendlin (1996) has poetically described this growth process in the following way:

...when a person's central core or inward self expands...it strengthens and develops, the "I" becomes stronger. The person--I mean that which looks out from behind the eyes--comes more into its own....

One develops when the desire to live and do things stirs deep down, when one's own hopes and desires stir, when one's own perceptions and evaluations carry a new sureness, when the capacity to stand one's ground increases, and when one can consider others and their needs.... One comes to feel one's separate existence solidly enough to want to be close to others as they really are. It is development when one is drawn to something that is directly interesting, and when one wants to play. It is development when something stirs inside that has long been immobile and silent, cramped and almost dumb, and when life's energy flows in a new way. (Pp. 21 - 22)[3]

The Focusing process is an operationalization of these beliefs, which correspond to a, b, and #1 above. Every "hang-up", every bad behavior, ugly feeling or unpleasant character trait is considered to be a manifestation of the growth tendency that has been blocked. Luckily it is not necessary to *believe* this in order to do Focusing; we simply act as if it is so. The longer we Focus, the more our experience bears out the hypothesis. Thus, when one of my Focusing clients, a school counselor, starts ranting angrily about the behavior of his young charges, I listen unperturbed and have no desire to ask him to be a little more objective or empathic, because my experience allow me to imagine what may,

---

[3]Gendlin, E.T. *Focusing-Oriented Psychotherapy cited in http://www.focusing.org/defining.htm*

and does, happen next: soon he takes a deep breath and says, "let me feel into that a little". His eyes moisten as he becomes aware of how personally he feels their behavior, how strongly he needs to see himself as a good counselor. Soon he says softly, 'It's not their fault. It's not their job to make me feel good about myself". He has been able to do this in part because years of Focusing have taught him to take *responsibility* (principle 3) for his behavior *and* his feelings. He can no longer see others as the cause of all his problems, as he did before he started Focusing.

A basic assumption of Focusing is that even though we may be seriously emotionally injured, something in us remembers "how it should be", and we listen to ourselves in a way that is consistent with this belief; the result usually justifies our faith. Thus, as we Focus on the pain and emptiness due to missing childhood love, through a series of emotional shifts, a felt sense of love develops. As Gendlin says, "What is missing fills itself in". When we feel stuck and blocked, we may ask our body what "fresh air" would feel like, and out of this comes forward steps of change. Thus experience shows us that "the healthy self is never destroyed" (principle b).

Focusing would also be impossible without principle c; we are the observer, the noticer, who recognizes our thinking (and feeling). Every Focuser starts out by learning to *notice, observe, or attend to* something that is stirring inside. Some of us describe this as finding *appropriate distance*. My colleague Ann Weiser Cornell, who brings her experience as a doctorally- trained linguist to her Focusing instruction, teaches her students to start Focusing with a phrase like "I'm noticing something in me that....". Thus we acknowledge a separation between an observing self and an experience. In doing so we leave ample room for *something else* also, so that the "something" that is angry can be accompanied by a something that is sad and a something that wants to heal. *I* listen and observe all these "somethings", trusting that as I name them, listen, and observe, they will develop in the direction of healing and growth. As in mindfulness meditation, no matter how deeply we may feel our experience, we also remain separate, rooted firmly in our observing selves.

Focusing listening usually takes place in a partnership. I listen to my inner places with empathy and respect, with the attitude that everything within has a good reason for being there, no matter how much I may wish it were not. We believe that humans always do the best they can with what they've got. If, for example, I dislike my passive-aggressive tendencies, I also know that they developed out of many experiences of powerlessness (or I may not know, but trust that there *was* a good reason). So I listen with empathy and respect, knowing that a healthier was of functioning will come, without my needing to force it. Just so my partner listens to me with the same empathy and respect, supporting me in the times when it is difficult to hold these attitudes. My partner listens attentively and carefully repeats back certain words, as I grope for a *handle for my felt sense.* I confidently "trust the unknown, waiting for fresh insights and out of the blue 'ahas' " (principle b). The relationship is supportive, Compassionate, and trusting toward both our insides and our partner.

In Focusing partnerships people are at their best, in certain respects. They must be empathic and supportive toward their partner, and honest, vulnerable, and non-defensive with themselves, or the Focusing does not work. Strong bonds develop under these conditions. Furthermore, as someone moves from story-telling and surface emotions down through deeper levels of meaning and feeling, they often seem to hit some near-universal human experiences. Quite often partners find themselves stirred by each other's disclosures, thinking (or saying) "me too". When a group of people comes together for Focusing partnerships, strong feelings of interconnectedness often develop, verbalized as a sense that "We are all in this together". Trust grows more quickly than in the average group and cooperative decision-making and mutual responsibility come more easily. Many people call this experience spiritual.

To be sure, the daily interdependence of a workplace or school is very different from a retreat or a weekly gathering. To what degree can cooperative decision-making function in settings in which real work must be accomplished? "In 1947, Carl Rogers gave up control of the Chicago Counseling Center. Student interns, secretaries and faculty ran it equally. Of course, involvement and productivity rose to new levels. Later, when the center lost its grant, this model showed its resilience: Everyone pooled their pay and worked for very little, until new funding was found. This was the Counseling Center to which I [Gene Gendlin] came as a graduate student in philosophy."4 Rogers also experimented with this approach in the classroom, with considerable success.

Few administrators even now have the courage (others would say poor judgment) to emulate Rogers. Nevertheless a Focusing program, we believe, can facilitate an environment containing "opportunities for participation and contribution that provide real responsibilities...a sense of ownership and belonging, and ultimately, a sense of spiritual connectedness and meaning".

Summary

Focusing teaches us to be the observer of our thoughts and feelings, knowing that we are far more than these. It teaches us to provide each other with caring,

---

4 Forward to Carl Rogers: The Quiet Revolutionary, An Oral History. Forward by E.T. Gendlin, http://www.focusing.org/gendlin_foreword_to_cr.html

supportive and empathic relationships that enable us to bring out the core healthy self that can never be destroyed. We are confident in "trusting the unknown, waiting and noticing fresh insights". Our personal reality changes and develops as our thoughts and feelings evolve. Out of this experience we often develop a sense of spiritual connectedness and meaning. In all these ways, Focusing training can contribute to resilience development and health realization programs in schools.

Trauma Facts for Educators

NCTSN

Child Trauma Toolkit for Educators | October 2008
The National Child Traumatic Stress Network
www.NCTSN.org

FACT: One out of every 4 children attending school has been exposed to a traumatic event that can affect learning and/or behavior.

FACT: Trauma can impact school performance.
• Lower GPA
• Higher rate of school absences
• Increased drop-out
• More suspensions and expulsions
• Decreased reading ability

FACT: Trauma can impair learning.
Single exposure to traumatic events may cause jumpiness, intrusive thoughts, interrupted sleep and nightmares, anger and moodiness, and/or social withdrawal—any of which can interfere with concentration and memory.

Chronic exposure to traumatic events, especially during a child's early years, can:
- Adversely affect attention, memory, and cognition
- Reduce a child's ability to focus, organize, and process information
- Interfere with effective problem solving and/or planning
- Result in overwhelming feelings of frustration and anxiety

FACT: Traumatized children may experience physical and emotional distress.
- Physical symptoms like headaches and stomachaches
- Poor control of emotions
- Inconsistent academic performance
- Unpredictable and/or impulsive behavior
- Over or under-reacting to bells, physical contact, doors slamming, sirens, lighting, sudden movements
- Intense reactions to reminders of their traumatic event:
- Thinking others are violating their personal space, i.e., "What are you looking at?"
- Blowing up when being corrected or told what to do by an authority figure
- Fighting when criticized or teased by others
- Resisting transition and/or change

FACT: You can help a child who has been traumatized.
- Follow your school's reporting procedures if you suspect abuse
- Work with the child's caregiver(s) to share and address school problems
- Refer to community resources when a child shows signs of being unable to cope with traumatic stress
- Share Trauma Facts for Educators with other teachers and school personnel

Psychological and Behavioral Impact of Trauma: High School Students
NCTSN

This project was funded by the Substance Abuse and Mental Health Services Administration (SAMHSA), US Department of Health and Human Services (HHS). Child Trauma Toolkit for Educators | October 2008 The National Child Traumatic Stress Network, www.NCTSN.org

There are students in your school who have experienced trauma.

Consider Nicole. Her teacher noticed that the tenth grader, who had previously been a very outgoing and popular student, suddenly appeared quiet, withdrawn, and "spaced out" during class. When the teacher approached her after class, Nicole reluctantly admitted that she had been forced to have sex on a date the previous week. She was very embarrassed about the experience and had not told anyone because she felt guilty and was afraid of what would happen.

Another example is Daniel. Daniel has become increasingly aggressive and confrontational in school. He talks throughout class time and has difficulty staying "on task." When approached by the teacher, his mother describes the constant neighborhood violence that Daniel is exposed to. He has witnessed a gun battle among gang members in the neighborhood and his mother suspects that he is in a gang. She is worried that he may be using drugs and alcohol. The mother also admits that during fifth grade, Daniel was placed in foster care due to physical abuse by his father and constant domestic violence in the home.

169

What do these two very different individuals have in common? They have both been exposed to trauma, defined as *an experience that threatens life or physical integrity and that overwhelms an individual's capacity to cope.* Generally traumatic events evoke feelings of extreme fear and helplessness. Reactions to traumatic events are determined by the subjective experience of the adolescent, which could be impacted by developmental and cultural factors. What is extremely traumatic for one student may be less so for another.

Some students show signs of stress in the first few weeks after a trauma, but return to their usual state of physical and emotional health. Even an adolescent who does not exhibit serious symptoms may experience some degree of emotional distress, and for some adolescents this distress may continue or even deepen over a long period of time. Some traumatic experiences occur once in a lifetime, others are ongoing. Many adolescents have experienced multiple traumas, and for too many adolescents trauma is a chronic part of their lives. Students who have experienced traumatic events may experience problems that impair their day-to-day functioning.

Be alert to the behavior of students who have experienced one of these events.

Be aware of both the adolescents who act out AND the quiet adolescents who don't appear to have behavioral problems.

These students often "fly beneath the radar" and do not get help. They may have symptoms of avoidance and depression that are just as serious as those of the acting out student. Try your best to take the adolescent's traumatic experiences into consideration when dealing with acting out behaviors.

Situations that can be traumatic:
• Physical or sexual abuse
• Abandonment, betrayal of trust (such as abuse by a caregiver), or neglect
• The death or loss of a loved one
• Life-threatening illness in a caregiver
• Witnessing domestic violence
• Automobile accidents or other serious accidents
• Bullying
• Life-threatening health situations and/or painful medical procedures
• Witnessing or experiencing community violence (e.g., drive-by shooting, fight at school, robbery)
• Witnessing police activity or having a close relative incarcerated
• Life-threatening natural disasters
• Acts or threats of terrorism

Self-Care for Educators
NCTSN

"There is a cost to caring." - Charles Figley
Resource: Figley, C.R. (1995). Compassion fatigue: Coping with secondary traumatic stress disorder in those who treat the traumatized. New York: Brunner/Mazel, Inc.

Child Trauma Toolkit for Educators | October 2008
The National Child Traumatic Stress Network
www.NCTSN.org

Trauma takes a toll on children, families, schools, and communities. Trauma can also take a toll on school professionals. **Any educator who works directly with traumatized children and adolescents is vulnerable to the effects of trauma**—referred to as Compassion fatigue or secondary traumatic stress—being physically, mentally, or emotionally worn out, or feeling overwhelmed by students' traumas. The best way to deal with Compassion fatigue is early recognition.

Tips For Educators:

1. Be aware of the signs. Educators with Compassion fatigue may exhibit some of the following signs:

- Increased irritability or impatience with students
- Difficulty planning classroom activities and lessons
- Decreased concentration
- Denying that traumatic events impact students or feeling numb or detached
- Intense feelings and intrusive thoughts, that don't lessen over time, about a student's trauma
- Dreams about students' traumas

2. Don't go it alone. Anyone who knows about stories of trauma needs to guard against isolation. While respecting the confidentiality of your students, get support by working in teams, talking to others in your school, and asking for support from administrators or colleagues.

3. Recognize Compassion fatigue as an occupational hazard. When an educator approaches students with an open heart and a listening ear, Compassion fatigue can develop. All too often educators judge themselves as weak or incompetent for having strong reactions to a student's trauma. Compassion fatigue is not a sign of weakness or incompetence; rather, it is the cost of caring.

4. Seek help with your own traumas. Any adult helping children with trauma, who also has his or her own unresolved traumatic experiences, is more at risk for Compassion fatigue.

5. If you see signs in yourself, talk to a professional. If you are experiencing signs of Compassion fatigue for more than two to three weeks, seek counseling with a professional who is knowledgeable about trauma.

6. Attend to self care. Guard against your work becoming the only activity that defines who you are. Keep perspective by spending time with children and adolescents who are not experiencing traumatic stress. Take care of yourself by eating well and exercising, engaging in fun activities, taking a break during the workday, finding time to self-reflect, allowing yourself to cry, and finding things to laugh about.

The Folio • Focusing Using Art With Adolescents

Barbara Merkur

On May 13, 1997 I introduced what I refer to as focusing-using-art to my graduating students of high school where I offer my 'Experiential Psychology' course. This was my way of bringing conclusion to the part of my program that deals with the emotions and mind/body integration. This school is an 'open school' which attracts students who are either partly employed and therefore cannot attend a full regular program or who, due to low self-esteem or apathy, might otherwise not have completed high school.

I prepared them for Eugene Gendlin's Focusing and discussed the research he conducted to determine why some clients improved through therapy while others did not, at least not as noticeably or quickly. I explained how his therapeutic approach was built upon a reconstruction of that natural process that many clients were undergoing on their own without any prompting from their therapists.

I emphasized that I was trying to find a way to use the art to facilitate this process and that I was going to experiment with my modified version of Gendlin's stylized technique to adapt to art therapy (I am a practicing expressive arts therapist who has completed my focusing training). I was hoping that they could help me refine the technique and understand the benefits, if any were evidenced.

The procedure I devised was as follows: To begin they were invited to make a picture of how they were feeling right now (as Laury Rappaport had done, Folio, 1988). I used this to help them get centered and in order to get them settled while we awaited the latecomers. (I dispensed with this for the second class finding it unnecessary overall.) A brief relaxation exercise followed to get them in touch with that inner part of themselves that is sensitive to their feelings, and then the notorious question: "Is there anything that is keeping you from feeling really wonderful right now?" I then proceeded, one by one to invoke each obstructing issue, their critic, and the background feeling, and asked them if they could represent these issues on the piece of paper which they had prepared at the beginning by folding it into eight equal divisions. Using the pastels I had provided for them, they were to label each issue that came to their attention, either through written words or images. This was to help them gain some emotional distance from these concerns, reducing their potency and size so as to direct them away from center stage. I reassured them that they could keep some with them if they felt a need to - as some already seemed uneasy to give up these identity attachments. I alerted those who might feel uncomfortable with cleared space, to instead concentrate on depicting those situations that occurred during the week that gave them energy (in order to help them fill their ensuing sense of emptiness). This relieved some of their concerns and provided an important option.

I then asked them to get a sense of that space inside (or for those others, for their space that now contained good energy) and then to depict it using the materials (finger-paints, chalk pastels, and oil pastels). Then I asked them to invite one of those things that was expressed on the eight squares onto a space on a new sheet of paper, the paper representing symbolically that cleared space. With finger-paints at their disposal and their excitement of using the bright colors and soothing texture, they were eager to explore how 'all of that' settled into that cleared space. Satisfied with the completion of their first murky picture, they were asked to find a word or expression that would capture the essence of that painting. I asked them to continue to elaborate creatively - either with the finger-paint or the other materials - whatever impressions had manifested in their picture; to stay with the feeling; and to continue to label that one and any pictures they made subsequent to the first, allowing that felt sense to get clearer or letting it take them to wherever it would lead. They were to ask, at those times when they sensed that something was feeling different in their bodies in response to what they had painted or drawn, what it is about that issue that made them feel so... (whatever the label word of the particular picture that brought this shift about was).

Many became very involved with this new space and felt a major shift just with this step. Some of them stayed with the good feelings and playfully used the materials to further express this newfound freedom. They were able to feel this 'new' sensation not only because they were using the finger-paints but also because many had divested themselves of their inner critic onto the page in the earlier process of clearing space.

Because there were only eight students in a group at one sitting, I was able to interact with each person for a short period of time to see how they were doing and to keep them from getting lost in a myriad of assignments. When a student would experience a new sense of the 'problem', I would help that particular student, encouraging him/her to ask of their picture image, what it was all about. Some of them felt a new incentive to deal further with their problem in answer to the response that finally emerged from their inquiry. For those who had no perceptible shifts, many felt empowered merely from engaging their problem with their full attention, something adolescents do not generally do. One student, however, who initially was reluctant to identify his problems, came away realizing and committing to the idea that his problems would have to be addressed at some future time. He felt more hopeful now that he was at least confronting them on the page, instead of denying their seriousness. I then asked those who had some time remaining, to paint how it felt to be with their new awareness and to write about their experience in their journals.

All the students underwent the process at their own pace and in their characteristic styles. One girl, who is a practical left-brain thinker seemed to move forward through the process but unfortunately could not yet connect her moving pictures with any body sensations. Despite the fact that her image transformed from the enclosed screen of her business computer that metaphorically spelled out her confusion, to a picture which expressed "excitement and release", she nevertheless, could not integrate the change as a physical release of tension. This inability to connect to her body reflects a tendency of hers to cut herself off from her feelings for fear that they might overwhelm her and thwart her overextended motivation. She is a workaholic and perfectionist whose only self-validated feeling is anger, a feeling many of the adolescents found particularly problematic.

By matching a word or phrase to catch the essence of what they had depicted in their art, they were able at each stage to make the shifts that were offering them a new way of being with their particular problem.

The completed processes which I have chosen to present, I feel, indicate the feasibility and effectiveness of this approach with adolescents. The first student is a withdrawn young man who is able to work things through the art much better than through words alone. He seemed very absorbed with the process and wore a confident smile upon completion of all the tasks. Something had evidently changed inside him with respect to how he felt about himself

The second student is a frail young man who has a habit of intellectualizing and one who had been skeptical about my self-growth program throughout the year. The finger-paints proved to be emotionally stimulating for students with this tendency much more than the more controlled media might have been. They somehow gave the student permission to be relaxed and to trust that something would evolve from their art of its own accord, much the way focusing inside will bring a felt sense if one learns to wait for it to come and have the faith that it will This student came away from this class feeling energized from the process. He was able to access the powerful energy of the archaic whale which came into focus in his cleared space. This dynamic energy brought him to some new awareness as he joyfully let it go through his creative process this day.

I have included write-ups from these two students that followed this whole procedure. Shifts were evident from their art, their words, the progression of their art from often closed structures to more open ones, amid from their more confident body language:

Student #1: He wrote: "After composing a list of the issues that were troubling me I was left feeling worse than when I started the exercise. On the reverse side I listed three things that I felt good about as you suggested for those of us who were having difficulty with the first part. I had a sense of relief from replacing my troubles with my more positive feelings. I realized that I needed to feel this relief. From the original list I chose to explore the troubles I was having with the future. I am finishing high school this year and my parents want me to choose a career path, i.e. university or other post-secondary education. I am unable to make decisions about my future. This inability has troubled me for some time and left me feeling lost and directionless. The feeling I get when I contemplated the future is my first finger-painting. I soon began to see my problem more clearly. While focusing on the problem and working with the paint, I began to see that my lack of immediate insight did not preclude a future decision. What I got from my final picture was not an ultimate solution, but a necessary reassurance that an answer will come."

One week later the above student wrote: "The partial solution I arrived at last week has helped me deal with other immediate problems. Using the finger-paints helped me realize that my lack of future plans was less pressing than some people had led me to believe. It helped that I had the chance to describe this with a friend. I have been better able to focus on immediate problems now. I have a lot of work I must complete before the school year ends. Now that I am not so preoccupied with the distant future I can address present concerns. Seeing my problem clearly has helped me set priorities and relieved some of my anxiety."

Student #2: This student journaled as follows: "The first picture, my 'Free Space' is represented by a whale, which always reminds me of something majestic. Also, the whale is full of energy. It has just dove back into the water and it is heading deeper, ever deeper. The black 'pillars' are my inner strength which holds everything up. I felt noticeably better after drawing this picture.

"My second picture is titled 'twisted' and it is just a big blob of tightness which is just there. It is incredibly tight and compact, as compared to the 'free space'. It is like the twisted wreckage of something.

"My third picture is titled 'The tree trunk is gnarled'. Gnarled is about two steps up on the 'twisted' scale. The picture is that of a tree trunk which is dead. The 'gnarledness' is something that I feel in my stomach. It happens when I'm tense. There is yellow which is representative of the sun rising over the tension to reach the stars. I think it is trying to tell me to deal with smaller chunks of tension instead of taking huge chunks which are unmanageable. The black hole is representative of the easy way through my tension. For me, black is representative of 'nothing new' which might just be the ticket to dealing with tension. Approaching it as though it were a hole in my life which keeps me from being whole. I felt that I have some new insight into myself, and how tension affects me."

A few months later I am still trying to assess the value of this entire approach with this adolescent population. It is important to realize that these students were gently prepared for such kinds of intervention through the experiential nature of this class and the progressive way it was structured to lead them past their defensiveness and general apathy to more openness and involvement. The art expression was much like a language that I facilitated in them, something innately theirs but much discouraged through traditional art education. Encouraging this form of expression, which embodies both unconscious and conscious material, is especially amenable for this population, allowing as it does, for them to remain private and therefore safe from being explicitly known by their peers in a group situation. Doing art spontaneously, i.e. without conscious direction, is not seen as threatening or intrusive, allowing the adolescent to relax in a meditative way, unimpeded by restrictive defenses. Using art in this focusing way brought them deeper into the process of knowing their potential and utilizing it in a fresh and self-directed way. In many ways I feel that this is the only way to ease these young adults into accepting focusing on its own merits, a process which I feel offers them, more than any other method, a way of acknowledging and being their real and separate selves, able to engage with others as confident and authentic. (It is important for me to

177

stipulate that anyone doing focusing-using-art with finger-paints, should be warned about the nature of this medium to stimulate kinesthetic memories for those who have experienced trauma.)

http://www.focusing.org/chfc

Incorporating Focusing Into the Classroom

Andrea Conway
The Folio, 1997

Editor's note: Although this article is written mostly about using Focusing in Catholic schools, almost all activities can be adapted to a secular context.

When I initiated focusing with my grade six class six years ago, I very cautiously introduced bits and pieces, and received such feedback as, "No offense, Mrs. Conway, but this is really boring!" It was those brutally honest comments that inspired me to seek more creative and fun ways of approaching focusing. Today, I take a far more holistic approach as I look to incorporate it in all the ways we live together in our class.

Focusing Environment

I work at creating a sort of 'focusing environment', both in and out of the classroom. It's a safe atmosphere - what Carl Rogers might call a student-centered environment, where all the necessary conditions of empathy, unconditional positive regard and congruence are found within the relationship between myself and the students. It is a place where teacher and student alike can risk being who we really are, not who we, or others think we should be.

It seems to me that this relationship must exist both in and out of the classroom.

Students must know that if there is a problem in the school yard or on the way home from school, I will listen. All too often, students hear from teachers that, "There's no point in telling me ... I can't do anything about something I didn't see." What nonsense! We can always listen, and we can always offer to stay with that child if he chooses to spend time with how it feels on the inside.

Focusing and Curriculum

I've looked for ways to make focusing a part of as many subject areas as I can, and I've also set aside time for planned activities. Certain subjects lend themselves to an attitude of body awareness of feelings and issues: Art, Music, Literature, Drama, Physical Education. It is quite easy to incorporate focusing into these subject areas and, as well, to enhance these subjects because of the increased body sense. Yet it is also possible to integrate focusing in all subject areas, without using all the traditional Focusing Steps. There are many examples of 'teachable moments' for focusing: first day of school jitters, pre-exam fear, excitement over a special event or school holiday, upsetting situations that occur, in or out of class time, feelings of boredom or stupidity.

As a teacher in the Catholic School System, I can incorporate focusing into any prayer situation-even on a school level. One of my roles is to encourage students to know God - to become more whole or more fully human. Yet the religious education programs tend to teach students about God, thereby encouraging the use of the intellect or head- brain as Campbell and McMahon refer to it. We must all - teachers and students alike - come to know God from within our body or our body-brain. If we experience who God is, and if we learn to recognize the body-feel of grace, then we will come to know God in our body, in everything we do, experience and feel.

I have found focusing useful on a one-to-one basis with students who are experiencing difficulties (or who are causing difficulties!). To date, I have used focusing with primary, junior and high school level students. I've had some enlightening and even exciting feedback from them, which has helped me in this process of bringing focusing into the classroom.

Long Range Plan

If Focusing is to be useful in my classroom, in any grade or subject area, then it must be part of my Long Range Plan. I try to include the following in this long range planning:

Teach about this special place inside ourselves where we can trust, find answers, and KNOW what is right for us. This knowledge is empowering.

- Remember that if I want students to trust me, then I must be trustworthy. Criticism erodes trust; sarcasm and ridicule kills it.

- With students, either individually or in a group, practice paying attention to how issues feel in our bodies. This doesn't have to take a lot of time.

- Learn to listen to these feelings in a caring way, even the feelings that are angry or very painful, because every feeling has something important to say and to teach us. Remember to be respectful if it is not okay to be with certain feelings and to listen to "not okay".

- Once we can get the feeling of the issue in our body, learn to wait and listen to its story.

- Take time with my students to be grateful, in whatever way feels right, for this gift of our bodies. Reinforce the importance of this gratefulness.

Focusing With Teens

Early last spring, I was invited to spend a half-day with forty-five high school students, in order to introduce them to Focusing. These students, ranging in age from 14-18 years, were spending their weekend at a Leadership Training Program, and I was well aware that many of them were hoping to combine learning with fun.

The workshop, entitled, Free To Be Me: Listening To The Story Inside, encouraged students to discover their "all-time favorite" ways of getting rid of their problems. It invited them to take a peek at the feelings that they tend to push away. Together we discovered how often our outsides do not match our insides and, finally, we spent time focusing as a group. I was overwhelmed by the oral and written feedback of the students, many of whom feel out of touch with their feelings and don't know what to do about it. Of the forty-five evaluations received, thirty indicated that they wanted to attend a workshop to learn how to Focus. The following is a sample of the comments received:

"This made me think about how I never let myself be sad. I can convince myself I'm happy and I will be, but the problem never gets worked out."

"I would have liked it if we could have gone a little deeper into the self focusing activity"

"Very beneficial for a 'lost generation' that doesn't really know themselves."

"I feel stupid. This is not a joke. I hate feeling stupid but I don't know how to deal with it"

This winter; I carried out a brief pilot project with a grade eleven Religion class of about 35 students. Our agreement was that if, at any point, they did not consider this personally useful, or if they were bored, then either I would not come back, or they would not have to attend this particular class. Well, they did have me back and they all continued to come to this class. Now, I might be tempted to attribute their enthusiasm to my 'brilliance' as a teacher, but I know that's not entirely true! The truth is that, while they did respond positively to my approach and use of humor; they were needing this look inside themselves. As one student wrote, "I found these sessions really helpful to feel free and get to know myself a lot better." Another commented, "I've been having a lot of problems and now I am learning how to at least try to deal with them. It's easier than wearing a mask."

The Elementary School Classroom

At the elementary school level I do not use the term focusing. I refer to "listening to the story inside", or "noticing how it feels on the inside". I often weave focusing through subject areas. For example, when teaching something about animals, I will create an opportunity to very naturally look at all the tender and gentle ways we relate to various animals. Naturally, this leads into the importance of caring about me and creating a caring-feeling presence within ourselves.

When I'm reading a story that the children are clearly enjoying, I'll be sure to stop at a critical point in the story so that the children are begging me to continue! This provides the opportunity next time we read together, to talk about something Marianne Thompson has spoken to her children about, namely, how it feels to be really engrossed in a story, the forward movement of the story, and wanting to know the ending. This, in turn, sets the stage for a further discussion on our own, personal stories and their forward movement.

Curriculum Exercises

During the past year and a half, I've been developing user-friendly materials for both primary and secondary students, and for both Catholic and public schools. I've found that much of the material works for any age, with minor alterations to language and approach. These exercises could fit into courses pertaining to self esteem, religious education, psychology. I have included a few sample activities on the following pages. Please note that I have added some comments that are intended as reminders for me, and may not suit someone else's style of delivery. Also be aware that these are 'works in progress' and are regularly altered with use.

General Comments

I am absolutely convinced of the tremendous need for focusing in our schools and in our classrooms, even though it is by no means a 'miracle cure' for children with emotional or behavioral difficulties. As well, there are many classes where focusing will never be a possibility, and this will not be determined by the subject area but rather by the teacher's openness to growth.

On the other hand, I believe that many teachers do create that safe environment where both teacher and student alike might risk being genuine, and might came to know more about who they really are. I look forward to any further pan I may play in this exciting process of bringing focusing into our schools.

Awareness Activity

This activity can be used, any time - to start off the afternoon, if there is a spare moment in the day, just before going home. It requires only one thing: quiet. This is an activity that may need to be repeated, and can help children with the whole concept of 'body awareness'. My grade 3/4 students thought it was fun!

Look at your hand ... keep looking at it.

Now close your eyes and notice if you can "see" your hand.

Feedback by children.

Look at their hand again ... keep looking.

This time, close your eyes and try to "feel" your hand.

Feedback. This is called your "awareness".

Let's take this awareness to other parts of your body.

This must be done without talking, otherwise the talking will interfere with the awareness...Look at your hand again ... keep looking. Close your eyes and "feel" your hand. Now try to keep your eyes closed and take your awareness to your wrists. Can you "feel" them? Take your awareness up to your elbows and notice if you can feel your elbows.

Open your eyes. At this point, you can ask for feedback - who could feel their wrists, elbows? Anything else they noticed.

Now we're really going to move!

Look at your hand. Close your eyes and feel it. Let that awareness move to your eyeballs - try to "feel" them. Let your awareness move to the tip of your nose. Can you feel it? (just answer in your head) Move your awareness to your shoulders. How do they feel ...relaxed, or tight, or maybe sore? Notice how they feel. Get ready ... because now you're going to drop your awareness right down to the bottom of your feet! Can you feel them? Finally, move your awareness to the skin between your big toe and the toe beside it. Can you feel it? Is it starting to get itchy? Very, very itchy? Don't you just want to scratch it?!!

Develop this game in whatever way works for you. When the activity has ended, have children share their experience. "What did you notice about your awareness? Was it difficult to move your awareness to certain parts of your body?"

(Adaptation from Gloria Bruinix)

God Invites Me To Be Gentle With Me

My feelings are part of my own special story. When I can become very quiet and still on the inside, and when I can stay with my feelings in a gentle way, then I can hear God telling me all about ME.

It's not always easy to be gentle with the feelings that I don't like, or with the ones that other people tell me are "bad". My teacher tells me that there are no "bad" feelings but that some feelings might seem "difficult". So, why do I feel "bad" when I feel them?

I need to remember something very important. When my best friend Mary was telling me her story about feeling really angry and jealous, I felt very caring toward her. I also thought that she was so brave to share such a difficult story with me. I felt special that she would trust me with her story. I really love my friend Mary and I know that God does, too.

Now .... can I be that gentle and caring with my very own story?

Draw yourself when you are being gentle and caring with your friend, a little baby, a special pet, or someone from your family

Getting Rid of Problems

RATIONALE: Most people utilize various strategies in order to remove or fix their problems and the accompanying pain.

INTRODUCTION: When! have a problem or some sort of difficulty that causes me inner pain or depression, I almost instinctively set out to remove the pain or to fix the problem. I'm amazed at how many different strategies I've perfected to deal with the pain and I frequently use more than one at a time! A few of my all-time favorite strategies for getting rid of my pain are ... (name a few!)

OBJECTIVES: To encourage self-awareness about the ways in which we avoid our pain and our problems. To encourage self-disclosure.

AGE/GRADE: Intermediate and high school GROUP SIZE: Maximum 30 students

MATERIALS: flip chart paper; markers, paper, masking tape, pencils

SETTING: Classroom or space with large floor space for sitting.

TIME REQUIRED: Approximately 30 minutes.

PROCEDURE:

1. As a group, brainstorm all the different ways or strategies in which we 'get rid' of our problems. Teacher will be looking for these kinds of strategies:

- Denial- I just pretend that everything is great; nothing's wrong. See my smile?

- Keeping busy - very, very busy with fulfilling and useful pursuits (Goes well with denial!)

- Escape- Let's not deal with it. The Escape routes are endless... excessive watching TY, reading, jogging, prayer, booze, drugs, sleeping, work, relationships

- God has often been used as the Great Fixer - If I pray sincerely enough and long enough, either God will fix my problem or I'll be too busy praying to notice it (Handy, because then if he doesn't, I have someone to blame!)

  Emphasize importance of both God and prayer; only you can know for sure if religion is being used to get rid of your problems--.

- Logical 'thinking it through', looking for solutions, finding excuses that justify the situation. (My baby left me because he was totally screwed up, and obsessed with his new guitar, he's a real loser - and so am I as a matter of fact. And now that I've figured out all the logical reasons, I can smile a lot and pretend everything is great, especially now that I'm jogging 10K seven days a week and I've taken on three more shifts in my job....).

2. With a partner (make sure no one is left out), discuss your favorite strategies for removing pain and list your two or three all-time favorites. You might come up with ones I haven't even used!

3. Large Group Sharing - As usual, share only what you feel comfortable sharing.

VARIATIONS: Each group of students could read a short story scenario, having to do with a 'real' teen issue. They would then examine and discuss which of their personal strategies they would generally use to deal with that situation.

This information would be shared with the larger group.

APPLICATIONS: This exercise is appropriate for any age group. Changes can be made to the level of language and the examples given in Procedure No. I.

DEBRIEFING/EVALUATIONS/FEEDBACK: Note what is happening in partner sharing and in large group sharing. Did anything emerge from this exercise that was especially helpful?

DANGER LURKING: Some students may feel that God and prayer are being 'put down', and may perceive a personal slight or offence. It is important to distinguish between such things as God's power and my using God to get what I want (my power), also the power of prayer versus the use of prayer to avoid problems.

FEELINGS ARE PART OF MY STORY

RATIONALE: We all experience many types of feelings. Some feelings have been deemed 'unacceptable' and so we determine to get rid of them. How we act might not match how we feel on the inside.

INTRODUCTION: All the different ways I act; all the different ways I feel: Do they match? Am I congruent? How often is how I act totally different from how I'm feeling inside? Am I being real and genuine? Am I being ME?

OBJECTIVES: - To review the many different types of feelings that we may experience. To become aware that the messages we receive through our heads are not always the same as the ones we receive through our bodies.

-To examine the notion of 'acceptable' versus 'unacceptable' feelings.

To introduce students to the notion of congruence

AGE/GRADE: Intermediate or high school

GROUP SIZE: Maximum 30 students, divided into groups of 4 students

SETTING: Classroom or space with large floor space for sitting

TIME REQUIRED: Variable

Exercise No. 1: 'NO NO' FEELINGS

MATERIALS: writing paper, pen or pencil, masking tape, flip chart paper, marker

PROCEDURE:

1. Teacher offers example of which feelings were 'not allowed' in his/her home when growing up (the NO-NO feelings). NO one had actually said they were not allowed - teacher just 'knew'

2. Students are invited to think about which feelings were or are 'not allowed' at their house.

3. Students may share their thoughts with the person next to them. Make sure no one is left out.

4. On a sheet of paper, list:

      a. Those feelings that were not allowed.

      b. The feelings that I usually push away.

5. Large group sharing and discussion. Student comments are recorded on chart paper.

NB. Notice if the 'not allowed' feelings are similar to the 'pushed away' feelings.

6. Question to ponder: If feelings are neither good nor bad, then how is it that some are deemed 'more acceptable' than others? If I don't accept all my feelings, then am I not accepting ME?

VARIATIONS: This exercise could include, What Feelings Are Not Allowed At School? or. With My Peers?

Exercise No. 2 Do My Outside Match My Insides?

MATERIALS: flip chart paper, marker for each small group, masking tape,

DO MY OUTSIDES MATCH MY INSIDES?

PROCEDURE:

1. Teacher briefly discloses an example or two of times or situations when how s/he felt on the inside was very different from how s/he was acting on the outside.

2. Students are invited to think of a time when their inside feeling did not match their outside behavior. Share with large group.

3. Students complete sheet, DO MY OUTSIDES MATCH MY INSIDES?

4. Large group sharing and discussion. Student comments are recorded on chart paper.

VARIATIONS: Students could list actions I do (e.g. smoked a Joint) versus how I felt inside (e.g. pressured and scared)

APPLICATIONS: These exercises can be use just as effectively with adults and younger students. Minor changes in language or situation examples may have to be made.

DANGER LURKING: Exercise NO. 2 could feel like a threat to someone who feels s/he needs to have that outer protective mask i.e.. "How I act on the outside".

BEAR IN MIND: Once again, bear in mind that all students are at their own stage of development and personal readiness for exercises such as these. Not all students will consider these exercises to be of value to them. While that is to be respected, at the same time, they must be respectful of the rights of the other students to partake in the exercises in a safe and 'put-down free' environment.

EVALUATIONS: Ongoing student feedback should be evaluated by the teacher, as an indicator of effectiveness. As well, students should be encouraged to offer ongoing feedback regarding such things as effectiveness, appropriateness and personal value.

DO MY OUTSIDES MATCH MY INSIDES?

All the different ways I act, all the different ways I feel: Do they match? Am I congruent? How often is how I act totally different from how I'm feeling? Am I being real or genuine? AM I BEING ME?

How I Act on the Outside How I Feel On the Inside

confident

goofy

timid/shy

tough

arrogant/ snobby 'cool'

happy

cheerful

INTRODUCTION TO GROUP FOCUSING EXERCISE

Before I begin this exercise of listening inside, I would like to say that it is a very gentle exercise that will take about 10 minutes. Feel free to participate or not - whatever feels right for you. All I would ask/insist, is that if you are NOT participating, you keep your eyes closed throughout the exercise out of respect for others. I really don't have any expectations of you and I want to assure you that there is no right or wrong way to do this. Whatever you experience will be just right for you -even if you seem to experience nothing.

Each of you should have a sheet to quietly complete at the end of the exercise. I would appreciate it if you could respond to the questions in some way. There is NO 'right answer' It may even be that you didn't experience anything, and that's perfectly OK. I'm not going to be disappointed!

The questions should only take a minute and then we will briefly share our findings if we wish with the person sitting beside us.

Following that, we will come back to the whole group. As usual, we will share only what we feel comfortable sharing.

BEFORE CLOSING THE EXERCISE, MAKE SURE EVERYONE IS OKAY!

"If anyone is feeling like they need to spend more time with an issue right now, I'm hoping you will honor that need. If you are comfortable letting me know, we can find a quiet place to talk..."

FOCUSING: LISTENING TO THE STORY INSIDE (EXERCISE)

I'm inviting you to close your eyes and to take a moment to grow quiet on the inside..

See if you can start to let your awareness move down into your body perhaps like water seeping into the earth. Just notice, "How am I feeling on the inside, right now ? Maybe I'm feeling really tired this morning. Maybe something happened at home this morning, or on my way to school (work). Or perhaps I have some feelings about being here right now... Maybe it has been a great weekend and I feel good about it. Maybe I'm feeling tense or tight or sore." Just take some time to notice how it feels on the inside right now.

Now, see if you can notice where in your body you can feel this. Ask, "Is it in my heart, or my eyes, or chest, or stomach, or my head, or just all over? Where is it?"

Ask yourself, "Is it OK to spend a bit of time with how I'm feeling inside? (pause...) If it's not OK, then that's the important part of my story right now, so...can I just gently be with that feeling of, "It's not OK."

Can I be gentle with myself and my story, and just as accepting as I would be with my friend who was telling me a difficult story?

191

Ask yourself, "Does that place inside need to tell me part of its story right now?" If it does, then take some time to listen. See if you can just be with it in an accepting way, rather than trying to fix it or push it away. Notice if something comes - a word or a picture, a symbol or a memory - something that seems to fit exactly how it feels inside right now...

Finally, let this place know that you may come back to it later tonight and spend more time with it... In whatever way feels right for you, give yourself a few moments to be grateful and respectful in this place of gift within yourself- perhaps in a way that says, "Thank you" to yourself.

When you are ready, you may gently open your eyes (and silently complete the questions on your sheet.)

FOCUSING: LISTENING TO THE STORY INSIDE

When you finish the focusing exercise, quietly complete the following statements:

1. When I grew quiet on the inside, I noticed that I was feeling

2. I could feel _____ in my _____my feeling) (part of the body)

3. It felt okay to be with that feeling.   YES NO (circle)

4. I needed to spend some time with the story behind my feeling.   YES NO (circle)

5. Comment

Teaching "Clearing a Space" to Elementary School Children, Ages 6-11

Mary McGuire, Psy.D.

Folio, Vol. V, Issue 5, 1986, page 148-160

The purpose of the Project was threefold:

1. To experientially check out my belief that most children naturally do what we call <u>Focusing</u>. The younger the child the more direct and unpretentious they are. They relate to a bodily felt place <u>inside</u> that knows when something feels right, when it doesn't. I was interested in seeing if there was a difference in how Grade I children (6 yrs. olds) related to their worries and problems as opposed to Grade VI children (10 & 11 Yr. olds).

2. To teach Clearing a Space as a Pilot Project to learn what difficulties are involved, how to sell it to the Principal, how to gain the cooperation of the Teachers, how much time is needed, what kind of follow-up and how to measure its effectiveness.

3. To teach children (who don't already know this) that they don't have to avoid their problems nor do they have to feel overwhelmed by them. By teaching them how to clear a space, the quality of their lives would be enhanced. This learning early in life how not to carry stress in their bodies could prevent stress related illnesses such as ulcers, migraine headaches, heart attacks etc. Also, by learning to listen to and trust that place inside that <u>knows</u> would lead them to greater self-control and a heightened awareness of their inner resources in problem solving. They would be more inclined to look inside for what is right rather than be

swayed by peers and others who think they knew what is right for children without valuing the child's feelings.

Introducing the Project to the School

It is important to spend time with the Principal and get him/her excited about Focusing. The Focusing Book and the literature on Creative Writing is helpful. You need to talk to the Principal in language that has value in education. For example, concentration, attention span, manner of answering questions, lest anxiety, behavior problems such as acting out their feelings. Once an atmosphere of openness and receptivity is created the Principal is the best one to invite the Teachers to participate. I use the word invite because only the Teachers who want to take part are given the experience of learning focusing. The principal leaves each teacher free. In this way if they participate it is because they want to, not because of pressure from above. If a spark of enthusiasm can be ignited in the teachers this will carry into the classroom where they will want to do focusing with the students because they believe in its value for learning.

Also, in speaking with the Principal be real clear about what you need. For example, how much time, room and space required, how many groups, equipment needed etc.

Since the teacher's role is crucial in this whole process you need to spend time with them. Teach them Focusing/listening; let them experience the benefits for themselves. After they have the process for themselves help them guide you through "Clearing a Space", give them encouragement and feedback. Talk over with them their feelings about doing clearing a space with the children each morning as they begin their day. Listen to their suggestions and through dialogue come up with the best way of carrying this out. It is important that whatever approach is decided the teachers feel comfortable with it.

Ask the teachers if you can be in the classroom with the children before you begin teaching them. Have the teachers fill in questionnaire on each student (See Appendix A). Let the children see you, feel you and let them show you their work. Children will intuitively sense your realness or lack of it. They need to feel you in their world and there can be no pretense about it.

What you say to them is not as important as what they feel from you without words. This is their criteria for connecting with you or not. For example, I worked with Grade I children making candles for Christmas, another day we built a snowman in the school yard. It was delightful to feel that free child space inside and just be with the children in play. I attended a basketball game with the

Grade VI students in which some of them played and the rest of us cheered and laughed.

Introducing Focusing to Grade I & Grade VI Children

I told the Grade I children that *I was going to teach them to listen to what they are feeling inside their tummy and chest and to let that feeling speak.* Then I said, *"Do you know that you can feel happy even when you are worried? And when you feel happy you can let that happy be felt in your whole body. It's like when you're playing and laughing ... where do you feel that?"* They answered, "all over, pointing to head, stomach & chest."

I asked them to bring their very favorite stuffed animal to class on Friday. There was much excitement and many questions such as can I bring my Cabbage Patch, my Care Bear, can I bring 2 in case someone forgets, etc? I asked them to bring something concrete that they loved because at this age children are very concrete and their attention span is short. Also, the sense of touch is heightened in young children. It is a deep communication.

Grade VI

I walked into the classroom and sat at a table at the back of the room. (The teacher and I decided that we would let them ask me questions rather than have introductions). After ten minutes or so, I walked around looking at what they were writing. They kept working as though I were not there. Then I went to the front and said:

"Hello, aren't any of you going to ask me who I am and what I'm doing here?" One boy asked and I said, *"before I tell you I'd like to know what you felt and where you felt it when this stranger walked into your classroom and walked around looking at what you were doing?"* One boy said, " 'nervous' like is she an inspector?" I said, *"where did you feel that nervous?"* He said, "in my stomach like butterflies." Another girl said, "I felt angry, like who does she think she is?" I said, *"where did you feel the angry?"* She said, "in my chest, when I get angry it gets tense in there." I said, *"can you feel the tense now?"* She said, "a little bit but it is getting more relaxed."

I then told them *who I was and that my purpose in coming was to teach them a skill that I believed would be of value to them.* I said: *"it will be like play, there are no exams, no grades and you can't fail."* Also, I shared with them that *I had asked for Grade VI specially.* They were very excited that their class had been chosen to be part of the project. *I had them tell me their names and one thing they wanted me to know about them.* When they had finished I said, *"It's not*

195

fair, I have twenty-six names to remember and you have only one." One boy answered, "well, you better stay after school and memorize them."

I then talked about *Focusing, how it started and its many applications. I spoke of Clearing a Space in terms of learning how to relate to their problems in such a way that they didn't have to run away from them nor did they have to sink in them and stay feeling down and sad. I said, "there is a middle way that I will teach you."* I explained that *this could help their attention span and concentration.* They asked many questions such as, "if I learn this will I have more energy?, will it help me sleep better and feel less pressure?, will it help me get along with my sister?, will it help me feel less sad about my Grandfather's death?"

They wanted to do it right away and after consulting with their teacher regarding time I lead them through some focusing exercises. I asked them *to get comfortable, put down pencils* etc. I explained that *focusing required being quiet inside and sensing one's body between their throat and lower abdomen.* I said, *"can you go inside and say a nice friendly, "hello" and ask how am I feeling right now?"* (silence). Then I asked if *anyone wanted to share what it felt like inside.* The answers were: tense, butterflies, soft, jittery, cramped, full and excited, nothing there.

Next I had them feel their big toe, without moving it, their leg, their thigh, lower abdomen, stomach and chest. Then I did some breathing exercises having them pay attention to their lungs as they breathed in and out. I then checked if they could have imagery by asking if they could see the bed they slept in last night. They all could. I asked them *for other imagery to get a sense of their capacity to know an imagery space.* They shared very rich imagery such as: one boy imagined himself flying the space ship to the moon, from his description and body gestures, it was clear that he was bodily feeling the thrill of this. Another girl shared that when she feels sad, she imagines herself sitting by a pond watching the stillness of the water and it feels peaceful inside.

Next, I talked about *"Clearing a Space" and how they could feel good inside even though they had worries and problems.* After discussion and questions we arranged a time to meet the following day. The library chairs were more comfortable and we could sit in a circle together.

The Experience of Clearing a Space with Grade I Children.

There were thirty-one children in the class. We sat in a circle on the floor in their classroom. I used their classroom rather than the library because I felt it better to keep them in familiar surroundings. I felt that this would create a more safe atmosphere for them. The children pushed each other to get close to me and two of the boys sat on my knee. They each held their stuffed animal and I had one too. I began by saying, *"I'd like us to get real quiet, maybe we could all close our eyes. I'm going to begin with asking you some questions like "when you feel happy where do you feel that?* I went through *excited, loving, peaceful, sad, angry, frustrated, left out, tense and anxious, asking where they felt those emotions.* They answered, in my chest, in my heart, in my tummy, (pointing). Then I said, "let's close our eyes again and see what you are feeling now. (silence) Answers: excited, warm, playing, laughing nervous. I asked one girl, *"where do you feel the warm?"* She said pointing to chest and stomach, "it flows all through here like the sun." The boy sitting on my knee said, "and what do you feel Mary?" I said, *"happy".* He said, "do you feel happy in here, pointing to chest? I said, *"I feel it like warm water flowing in here"* (chest & stomach).

Next, with each child holding their stuffed animal I asked them *to cuddle the animal and to feel their loving it inside, and to let loving go through their whole bodies.* There were smiles, their little faces shone with pleasure and joy as they caressed their animals (silence 2 minutes or so). Then I said, *"keep your eyes closed and stay with the feel of loving your animal." Now see if there is something you are worried about and if you find something see how that feels inside. Then take that worry and put it in your secret hiding place. Do you all have one of those?* I purposely asked this question because I intuitively believe that children know such a place. They answered "yes." After you do that hug the animal again and get the feel inside as opposed to the feel of when you are worried. (silence).

Take each little worry and put it in your secret hiding place. Then go back to cuddling your animal. Notice how each feels. It won't be long before I'll let you open your eyes and talk, just a minute or so. (One could visibly see the different body gestures and expressions when they were with the feel of a worry as opposed to a loving place).

We stopped and there was much sharing. They could feel <u>inside</u> and when I kept asking *where did you feel that*, the same little boy who was sitting on my knee said, "did you come all the way from Chicago to ask those stupid questions, everybody feels in here (pointing). Their imagery was very symbolic and notice I did not check out if they could have imagery. Examples of where they placed their worries: in their tree house, wrapped them in a blanket, in their mother's apron pockets, in a safety box in her room that only she has a key for, among her dolls in the closet, in Grandma's house, etc. It struck me that all of their imagery places were loving, soft, friendly and gentle. (As you will see this was not as prominent with the Grade VI students). There was much rich sharing and the children really enjoyed the experience. It was an energizing experience for me and I left their classroom feeling enriched and lifted by them. There was no doubt in my mind about these children's ability to focus. They sang a song they and the teacher had composed for me.

The Experience of "Clearing a Space" with Grade VI Children

We formed a circle in a big colorful room in the library. Some of the children sat in chairs and others sat on the floor. There were twenty-six students.

I talked about *the importance of feeling in a "safe atmosphere."*

I explained that *when it came time for sharing that I wanted them to check inside if they felt comfortable sharing. If they didn't, they could say "I pass."* With this understanding we could go around the circle so that everyone who wanted to share would have a chance and yet no one would feel pressure to do so.

I asked them *to get comfortable, some of them took off their shoes.* They had rushed in from recess so we began with breathing exercises to help them come down and get quiet inside.

I asked them *to put their attention inside somewhere between their throat and lower abdomen and to say a nice friendly "hello" once they were there.* (Silence, to give them time to do that). *I want you to ask in there, "how am I feeling right now? What is in the way of my feeling all ok? (silence). When a problem or a concern comes up, see what feeling it gives you in your chest or stomach and then place it in an imagery space outside of you* (silence). *When you have done this, take a deep breath and sense if it feels any different inside, like is it even slightly less tight?*

Then ask, now do I feel Ok or is there something more? Again, if something comes, be with it for a minute, then place it in an imagery space outside of you (silence).

We did Clearing in this manner with four or five times of checking inside to see what was in the way of feeling all ok. Then I asked them *to check if there was a background feeling, something that was always there. Again, I asked them to place it out.*

After having them *stay with this Clear Space for a few minutes enjoying its quality I asked them to pick something they love, not a person nor a pet.* Then I asked them *to let a body felt sense come inside of their loving that thing. And that they may get a word or an image to help them to hold onto it.* (silence). I

198

instructed them *to ask what is it about that that gives me this freeing or whatever their quality word was*. I asked them *to let the feel of whatever came flow through their whole inner space* (silence).

I told them we would stop in a few minutes.

The reason I had them Clear a Space and then choose something they love, I wanted to give them an experience of focusing on something positive. I wanted to teach them that focusing isn't only for processing problems. Yet I felt it was important to teach them to work on a problem that they promised to pay attention to at a later time. We discussed this, and they asked that we have a time to practice how to work with a problem using focusing. What was interesting about this was that because of their class schedules I worked with half the group at a time. The children remarked how much better it felt with a smaller group. They felt safer and it was easier to be with whatever came inside.

The following were shared by the children from their experience of Clearing a Space:

1. I placed it under my mattress (it's a problem at night) I'm on top of it and I feel strong about it, it doesn't get me anymore. He says he has it under control of him and that feels different (laughs).

2. He and the problem go up the ski-hill together on the chair-lift. He leaves it at the top of the hill and he skies down. Then he sits at the bottom and glances at it. He feels inside a lightness, not the heavy black that was in his stomach before. Then he laughs saying "but if I can't go back up the hill because it's there it still has me, right?" It's controlling my fun and that's not right. I said, *"check and see what would feel right?"* (silence). He said, "1 can go up another hill and have fun. I'll leave it there then I can enjoy myself. (laughs). I'll glide down saying ha, ha, I'm in charge of you. (laughs).

3. He imagined his problem as a hockey puck. He beats it around, then has it drop down the hole in the goalie; he skates off feeling free and says, "I have a big laugh inside me; I'm in charge of you; you only think you got me."

4. She imagined she was flying to Florida; she is feeling weighed down with this problem and can't relax - she imagined herself getting off in Toronto and let the plane take her problem to Florida - she said, "It now feels like a glow inside and light."

5. Boy said, "I took my problem down-stairs and placed it in the walk-in freezer; I closed the door and went upstairs. I wanted it to feel cold because that's the

way it feels in my stomach "cold lump". It felt good inside when I closed the fridge door. But when I got upstairs, it was right back cold in my stomach again. It wouldn't stay there. I said, *"can you feel it in your stomach now?"* "Yah, cold lump, it's there whenever this problem is here."

I said, *"maybe it needs something from you before you place it. Can you check and see if that's right?"* (Silence). "Yah, it's scared that I'll forget it." I said *"be nice to the scare; see what's so scary?"* (Silence). "It needs me to promise I won't forget it, that when I get home from school take it out and give it some attention."

I said, *"can you promise it that?* (silence) - "yah, if it leaves me alone during the day. - (silence, breath), he said, "I put it in a blanket in the fridge and promised I'll take it out for awhile after school. Big breath, (laughs) now it feels like I can breathe." It really grips me when it's inside, that feels different (laughs).

6. Girl imagined each problem as a little fish - they swam out in the lake when she told them to; she stayed on the shore; it feels big inside me when they were gone, but it didn't last; they all came back. Then I had this big Clam; I opened it and I had all the little fish swim into the Clam,

then I closed it so they couldn't get out again. It felt like a breeze inside me. I then lay on the beach; the Clam was beside me but I could feel a freedom; the sun's warmth glowed in my stomach because all my problems were in the Clam. I was free of them. Isn't that weird, how that is so different when they are not in me. (laughs) - I think I'll just carry around the Clam and keep my problems in it, then I can be happy - (big smile & sigh).

7. Girl placed problems in different pages of a book on her book-shelf at home and then closed the book. She said, "I usually take the book and look at it once a week; I can look at those 3 problems then. Do you think that would work?' I said, *"I'm not sure, can you ask inside if that is right?"* (silence) - she said, "something is nagging me and I don't know what it is." I said, *"be gentle where you feel the nagging; just be with the nagging"*- (silence). She said, (smile) "I need to put them in different books, because when I open the book, they will all come out at once and I can't handle that. I need to look at one at a time". I said, *"can you place each one in a different book now?"* (long silence) "I put two of them in different books (sighs) and that's better, but the one that bothers me most is too big to stay there." I said, *"ok, take your time and sense inside; let your inside place tell you where to place the big one."* (silence) "At home we have a roat cellar with a big door to the entrance; I'll place it in there." I said, *"ah, can you do that now?"* (silence), "yah, (breath) it's there all right (laughs) - I said, *"what is it like inside now?"* She said, "roomy" (laughs).

Some of the quality words they shared from the experience of the love exercise were: invigorating, a gentle breeze, like sunshine, warm all over, excited, freeing, I imagined a garden being watered it felt clean and warm. My work with the children gave me a feeling of being connected with life in all of it's splendor and beauty. I left feeling like I had received a gift.

Conclusion & Implications for Research:

This preliminary study taught me much about setting up and carrying out a research project with school children. It was a warm joyful experience for me as I felt welcomed by the Principal, Teachers and children. I worked with three teachers, teaching them Focusing/Listening and especially how to Clear a Space. These teachers taught Grade I and 6. My intent was to have them do this with the students after I left. I was in the school for one week. I spent much time in the teachers lounge. I didn't push anything but I put focusing books and literature on the tables. The teachers asked many questions and many of them wanted to experience the process.

There is a real need for research in this area. Clearing a Space using the same instructions and measures for the various ages, and monitoring similarities and differences. For example, I observed that the younger children placed their worries in loving places. (Was this because I said, "your secret hiding place?") Whereas, with the Grade VI children I said, "an imagery space outside of you." I don't know the answer but it raises some interesting questions. The same instructions would have to be given to both groups.

The Grade VI children seemed to have more of a need to be in control than the Grade I children. Their examples from Clearing a Space indicates this. Also, while over half of the Grade VI children seemed to have little difficulty with the process, others had problems feeling anything inside.

Many research projects could be initiated such as: Focusing and Creative Writing with school children. This project was not set up with a clean research design. I did have a pre - and post questionnaire for the teachers to fill in.

They filled in the pre-questionnaire (Appendix A) but not the post-questionnaire.

The Teachers needed much more support than I was able to give them.

I visited the school 8 months after my initial visit. The Teachers had practiced it occasionally with the students but not on a regular basis. The school was located in Ontario, Canada and much more support and involvement would be needed to keep the project alive. Also, I could see a real need to form groups of Teachers who focus and listen to each other. Also, children's groups depending on their age could be set up and once they really had learned Focusing/Listening they could pair with each other and the Teacher and/or Parent could be used for consultation when they had difficulty. Also, parents could be taught the process and involved in groups. What a different school and community spirit would develop as more and more people get involved!

Thomas Merton (1979) says, "The danger of education is that it so easily confuses means and ends. Worse than that, it quite easily forgets both and devotes itself merely to the mass production of uneducated graduates - people literally unfit for anything except to take part in an elaborate and completely artificial charade which they and their contemporaries have conspired to call "life". (p. 10).

In closing I want to quote from a song that is very meaningful for me.

"I believe the children are our future. Teach them well and let them lead the way.

Show them all the beauty they possess inside

Give them a sense of pride". (The Greatest Love of All).

References: Merton, Thomas, Love and Living, Edited by Naomi Burton Stone and Brother Patrick Hart, Bantam, 1979

Listening: A Key Skill in the Training of Teachers and Human Services Personnel

Fernando Hernandez, Ph.D.

For more than 35 years I have been a professor of education at California State University, Los Angeles. During that time I have taught classes in human development, counseling, educational psychology, learning theory and the like. I enjoy all of my classes and delight in the thought that I am preparing teachers, counselors and other human service professionals to help their fellow human beings grow and develop. Teacher training has been the primary focus of my work.

The principle aim of the courses that I have taught is to help students understand those processes that are part of the growth and development cycle of the human being. Of particular interest is learning and behavior. Helping people to learn as well as to understanding their behavior is no easy task. Teaching, counseling and helping people to help themselves requires quite a bit of skill and training if one is to be effective. Thus I spend lots of time teaching the many important thinkers in psychology, including Freud, Erikson, Maslow, Rogers, Skinner and others so very important to an understanding of human psychology.

For much of my career I was content to just lecture and give exams, then later as I matured as a professor I began to involve my students more by asking them to give group reports and mini-lectures on the material covered in my courses. Still there was a vague sense of dissatisfaction with all of this as I wanted the material to penetrate my students' thinking more deeply. I wanted to develop not just good practitioners, but along with that, my goal was to help form reflective practitioners. Practitioners that constantly reviewed what they were doing, with the aim of continually improving their practice.

We all know of persons in the helping professions that know the theories and principles of good psychology but cannot put those things into practice. What became obvious to me was that this required more than just good didactic training, but personal development as well. If we are to help people get in touch with themselves, we also need to be in touch with ourselves. Focusing has helped me to understand my teaching better and has been a great aide in stimulating me to change the way I now teach.

I teach focusing as part of my courses. The reason is quite simple; I want my students to not only read psychology but to live it as well. And, while we have much to learn about what it means to be human, there is much that we have discovered about human beings that can be of great use to all of us. The great theorists have helped us to look at ourselves in ways that provide us insights into what we and others can do to develop more positive, productive ways of living.

But therein also lies a challenge, how to make these sometimes abstract theories connect to real life, my students' lives in particular. One way is to put into practice some of what we have learned. Here is where I have found the work of Eugene Gendlin of great benefit. Gendlin has both a theoretical base founded on sound principles of humanistic psychology as well as a process or technique to help a person get in touch his/her life that helps connect the person to core issues related to his/her life.

In teaching Focusing I rely on Gendin's six step approach found in *An Introduction to Focusing: Six Steps* (Gendlin, 1996). I have found that this is an easy to read, understandable tome that lays out a sequence of steps that are easy to follow and learn. I first introduce them by doing some guided practice and also using two Youtube videos , *Eugene Gendlin Introduces Focusing Pt1* (Gendlin, 2000a) & *Pt2* (Gendlin, 2000b). I also do a short practice with a student volunteer where I lightly touch on the process without going too deeply into personal issues. I make it a short 10 to 15 minute session. Here I emphasize the importance of listening as a process.

Listening as I teach it is a dynamic process that involves both the person being listened to and the listener. What is most important for me in this process is the importance of listening to what the other person is saying, how that person is saying it and what sense is being conveyed in the process. Equally important is how I am receiving the communication, with a special effort not to inject my values, goals, opinions or prejudices into the process. During the guiding practice I do with the students, I also teach listening, by asking students to learn to listen to themselves, and very prominently to also learn to listen to their body. Listening done in this manner becomes a whole body experience not just a mental activity.

Eventually, I put the students into pairs, which is done by asking students to find someone they would like to work with. For the most part this works, but if need be I will help someone find a partner. Where students are absent or where there is an odd number I will work with the odd one out. Once this is done I set aside about a half an hour toward the end of class to give each student a chance to "check in" with one another. This I have found a good approach as students can give one another more time if needed. Also, during this time I walk around and observe students working together. I note what I observe and hear so that I may share my impressions with the class the next time we meet.

I have found real listening is not an easy skill to learn. In fact most of my students when first asked almost always thought they really knew how to listen. By the end of the course when they submitted their final class reflections, almost all had changed their minds and reported that they had been mistaken. Almost to a person they reported struggling to really listen without judgment or prejudices. They also reported how hard it was for them not to jump in and give advice as opposed to good feedback. Listening they found, required practice and commitment. Moreover, in talking to many of my students throughout the course I found that the many mistakes they made in listening to others they also made in listening to themselves. Focusing requires listening to both ourselves and others.

As we learn to listen to ourselves, openly, in a caring and loving manner, it becomes easier to do so with others and vice versa. Thus, as we learn to listen to others in a manner where we are really trying to get a feel for and a clearer picture of what the other person is experiencing, we are at the same time becoming more capable of doing so with ourselves. This, I think, is the importance of interaction as a process in Focusing. Interaction, coupled with feedback and reflection makes for a very powerful combination.

There is another aspect to the listening process that is particularly salubrious, and that is the power that it provides the person. Perhaps a better way of putting it is that Focusing puts persons in touch with the power in others and the power within. What I found with my students was that they were most often not very trusting of their own feelings or their ability to understand their own lives. I suppose some of this comes from the societal predisposition to worship experts or gurus. With Focusing you become your own guru. The power to access our own feelings and make sense of them with both mind and body is something I believe we all can do. With some it takes more time and work, with others it comes easily. Focusing nevertheless is a powerful process that taps the power we all have to live life in a manner that is more congruent with who we really are, to find what it is we really need, to tap into how we really want to be. Once tapped the power-to-be becomes possible. External forces become more manageable and better understood. We are as a result less anxious, less stressed and more open to change in our lives. Life then becomes a process of choices that either fit or do not fit who we really are.

Here are some of the comments I received from students about listening:

"Listening was a big topic in this class, as well as it is in everyday life. [I found] Being listened to be very helpful, it made you feel good. We had to talk for 20 min, and having someone there to listen without being interrupted made you feel warm. Listening took a while to figure out because, to listen it means not to interrupt. "

Another said:

"I have learned that I cannot ever really know what a person is experiencing, but through the focusing exercises I have learned to listen to what a person is actually saying to help them evaluate and solve their own problems. My listening and attentive skills have made much progress since the beginning of class. The first focusing exercise was horrible. My partner and I just had a conversation. I found it very difficult to put my own interests aside and listen to the other person. I also found it hard to share my feelings and thoughts with the other person. By the last exercise I already felt comfortable to share everything right away with my partner; and we both were able to put our own issues aside and really listen to one another."

This student gives an insight into his learning with respect to listening:

"I really loved doing our focusing practices in class with our own personal reflection times that the professor conducted and also being able to listen and talk with our focusing partner on a weekly basis. I believe that being able to develop these skills is something that will stick with us and help us for the rest of our lives. Being able to listen effectively is a skill that a person needs to be successful in life in my opinion. It is a skill that is needed in school, in relationships, and in careers. From a personal standpoint, my skills in this area greatly improved as the quarter developed. I was able to change my ways from wanting to talk and throw in my opinion while listening to just sitting and listening and really connecting with my partner. It is a skill that I tend to keep developing and improving on past this class. So being able to develop and practice these skills was something that I believed was the most important and best part of this class."

There were more, much like those above, but I can say with confidence that this part of the class was found to be helpful by just about every student. Given that these students are on their way to becoming teachers, counselors or entering some type of helping profession it was clear to me how little they knew about effective listening. It seems everyone thinks they know how to listen, but there is certainly an important distinction between hearing a person and listening to him.

In sum, one of the most essential elements to Focusing – listening, had a powerful effect on the students in my class in a number of ways. First, it taught them to more effectively interact with their fellows. Second, it enabled them to practice empathy by gently forcing them to try to get in touch with how others were feeling. Third, it taught them the importance of checking in with their own feelings. Fourth, it helped them to listen to themselves more clearly. And finally it helped them to understand the power that all human beings have to create movement in their own lives in a way that is more congruent with who they really are. The time and effort that we all put into this aspect of Focusing has paid off handsomely for both my students and for me personally. I have the satisfaction of knowing that through my course they have acquired a new set of skills that they will be able to use to help themselves and others throughout their lives.

References Cited:

Gendlin, Eugene. YouTube - Eugene Gendlin introduces Focusing (Pt.1 International Conference Toronto 2000a). http://www.youtube.com/watch?v=j7PEC5Mh5FY.

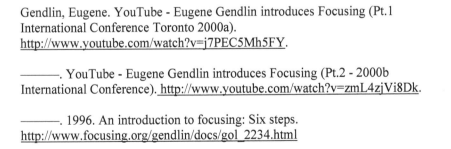

————. YouTube - Eugene Gendlin introduces Focusing (Pt.2 - 2000b International Conference). http://www.youtube.com/watch?v=zmL4zjVi8Dk.

————. 1996. An introduction to focusing: Six steps. http://www.focusing.org/gendlin/docs/gol_2234.html

Checking in with Yourself
A Biospiritual Practice That Builds Body-Links of Hope Into The Hidden Story-Connections Within Your Feelings

Edwin McMahon, Ph. D.

The purpose of this Check-In during your day is to develop a habit of noticing and nurturing your important feelings. A story lies waiting to be heard inside what your body already knows about your life, even before your mind can ever think it. This knowing in your body is different from thinking in your mind. The Check-In allows body knowing and head knowing to begin working together.

NOTICING

1. Growing Quiet and Going Inside

Take a moment to close your eyes and allow the chatter in your head to die down by letting your awareness settle into the center of your body, and noticing how you feel there.

Pause and take some time to do this.

When you're ready ask yourself: "Is there any important feeling inside me right now that needs listening to? It can be one that's easy to be with or one that's difficult. Notice where you carry this feeling in your body and <u>how</u> it feels.

Pause to do this.
NURTURING.

2. Caring for How Your Body Carries This Feeling.

Without trying to change or fix anything, or think about it, take some time right now to stay with how it feels to be carrying this in your body.

Let this feeling place know by your presence, that you are with it, that you care, and that you are open and listening if it has something to tell you.

If it helps, put your hand on the place where you carry this feeling, letting your hand say, "I am here. I care. I am listening."

Pause.

Take your time, and sense whether anything comes inside-like a word, image, a memory, or feeling-that seems to fit or connect with how it feels to be carrying this in your body.

Pause.

GOING FURTHER WITH NOTICING AND NURTURING.

3. Recycling.
Whenever something fresh or new, unexpected or surprising comes inside, notice and <u>stay with the new feeling in your body</u>. Be caring and gentle with how your body carries this new felt edge that came when some word, image or memory, etc. connected with how it feels inside.

Sense whether anything further comes inside for you, like another word, image, memory or feeling, that seems to fit or connect with what you now carry in your body.

Pause.

Continue to repeat numbers two and three as needed.

ENDING A SESSION

Checking to See Whether It's OK to Stop

1. Ask yourself: "Does this feel like it wants to unfold a little further at this time, or would this be a good place for me to rest and stop-at least for now? "

2. Whenever it feels right to stop, allow yourself a few moments to remember how it felt when you first began being with your feelings, noticing how it felt to be carrying that feeling in your body. Then notice how it feels inside right now. Does it feel the same, or is there any difference?

Pause.

If it feels the same, go to (1) below. Otherwise, close with number 3.

3. For a moment, allow yourself some time to be quiet and grateful for the gift of this new relationship to yourself. (*Pause*) if it feels right, promise that you'll come back at another time to go further. Then, when you're ready, bring your Check-In to a close.

Pause.

Stopping in an Unfinished Place.

1. When you need to stop in an unfinished place, ask the feeling that still has more to say

"How do you need me to be with you so you can be my friend and teacher?" Give yourself a quiet moment to listen for direction from inside your feeling.

Pause.

2. Also, promise this place that you will come back at another time, so it can continue to tell you more of its story. .

Then, end your Check-In with number 3 above.

It might help to look upon your body's knowing. like the layers of an onion. As each layer is revealed, a little piece of your inner story seeps into awareness. The stories, however, are all about connections, linking. It is the way you are tied-in to people, places, events, and time. Thinking is only a very small part of your conscious world. Felt connections are what influence most of our lives. We are linked into our personal histories, and into a much larger world of gift and grace-- which will continually surprise us, if we allow it to do so.

Helping Someone with a Check –In
Edwin McMahon, Ph.D.

The companion's role is to be a "caring presence", encouraging a person to stay in their body, noticing and nurturing important feelings, so their hidden stories can surface. Your role is <u>not</u> to give advice, analyze, or comment upon what they find. Privacy is always respected. It is not necessary for them to share the content of their feelings, unless they choose to do so.

"Bold text in quotes..." below is what you say to the person you are companioning. (*Italic texts in brackets...*) are instructions for you.

Set up simple ground rules for responding back to you by saying, **"As I give you directions, I will repeatedly say: 'Let me know if something comes that fits the way this feels'. You can respond with a nod, an OK, or say something more if you wish."**

NOTICING

1. Growing Quiet and Going Inside

"Take a moment to close your eyes and allow the chatter in your head to die down by letting your awareness settle into the center of your body and noticing how you feel in there."

(Pause)

"When you're ready, ask yourself: 'Is there any important feeling inside me right now that needs listening to?' It can be one that's easy to be with or one that's difficult. Notice where you carry this feeling in your body and how it feels. "

"Let me know if you find such a feeling."

(Pause)

NURTURING

2. Caring for How Your Body Carries This Feeling.

(When the one you are companioning finds something, invite them to be with it as follows:)

"Without trying to change or fix anything, or think about it, take some time right now to stay with how it feels to be carrying this in your body.

(Pause)

"If it helps, put your hand on the place where you carry this feeling, letting your hand say, 'I'm here. I care. I'm listening, if you want to tell me something.'"

(Pause)

"Take your time, and sense whether anything comes inside-like a word, an image, a memory, or feeling-that seems to fit or connect with how it feels to be carrying this in your body."

(Pause)

GOING FURTHER WITH NOTICING AND NURTURING

3. Reflection.

(Say back whatever the one you are companioning shares. Use his or her words-not yours! If they say a lot, reflect back only the most feeling part.)

4. Recycling.
(Whenever something fresh or new unexpected or surprising comes inside, invite the person to notice and stay with the new feel in their body.)

For example: "Take some time, now, to stay with <u>the body feel</u> of what just came and felt connected for you. Try to be open and caring with how your body carries this new felt edge of an unfolding story."

"Let me know if anything further comes, like a word, image, memory or feeling, that seems to fit or connect with what you are now carrying in your body."

(Pause)

(Continue to repeat numbers three and four as needed.)

ENDING A SESSION

(a) Checking in to See whether it's OK to Stop.

1) "Ask yourself: 'Does this feel like it wants to unfold a little further at this time, or would this be a good place for me to rest and stop-at least for now?"

(Pause)

2) *(If they want to stop, say:)* "For a moment before stopping, recall how it felt a little while ago when you first began being with your feelings, noticing how it felt to be carrying that feeling in your body. *(Short pause)* Then notice how it feels inside right now. *(Short pause)* Does it feel the same, or is there any difference? Let me know what you find."

(Pause)

(If they say, "the same." Then go to #1 below. Otherwise close with number three.)

3) "For a moment allow yourself some time to be quiet and grateful for the gift of this new relationship to yourself. *(Pause)* If it feels right, promise that you'll come back at another time to go further. Then, when you're ready, you can stop."

(b) Stopping in an Unfinished Place

1) "When you need to stop in an unfinished place, ask the feeling that still has more to say: 'How do you need me to be with you, so you can be my friend and teacher?' Give yourself time to listen for direction from your feeling."

(Pause)

2) "Also, promise this place that you'll come back, so it can continue to tell you more of its story."

(Pause)

(Then close with number three above.)

AFTER A SESSION

(Ask:) "Is there anything you'd like to share from this experience, or would you rather just be quiet?"

Dr. McMahon can be contacted at the Institute for BioSpiritual Research.

The Institute and its members do not teach the habit of noticing and nurturing important feelings as a substitute for professional psychotherapeutic or psychiatric care for those who need it, nor as a substitute for training and licensing in the above health fields.

APPENDIX

Going Ahead With Focusing

Lucinda Gray, Ph.D.

Focusing is an experiential process, not something you can master by simply reading about it, or even being guided through it a few times. But don't be discouraged; because you will find it more rewarding every time you sit down to spend time with yourself in this special way. As you practice the method and become more fluent with Focusing it will change your life in wonderful ways. You will be more accepting of your own humanity, all your perfection and imperfection; you can even learn to love your faults as natural parts of you. As you work the Focusing process your sense of self will expand to include so much more of all that you are.

The best way to learn Focusing is with the help of a teacher, either in individual sessions or in small group classes. Many of the contributors to this book offer classes, workshops and /or individual sessions. I usually recommend 6 to 8 individual sessions for the ideal learning experience. With individual training you have the opportunity to work on your own personal issues in a confidential relationship with your teacher, while you are learning how to use the steps of the Focusing process. Classes and workshops have the advantage of being less costly. Many teachers offer classes remotely via phone or Skype, so that you don't need to leave your own home.

Focusing can be practiced either by yourself or with a partner, but it is much easier to Focus in partnership. A partner provides a tracking observer who can

219

reflect back to you what you are saying, help you return to your body sense, or help you to hear the key words you used that point to the Felt Sense.

There is something magical about being listened to in the careful, gentle non-judgmental way of Focusing. We want to encourage you to explore the possibilities of Focusing by seeking out a Focusing partner. Maybe there is someone special in your life, a partner or friend who you would like to introduce to Focusing, so that you could practice together. Being Focusing partners can deepen your relationship. It helps you to take an accepting attitude that fosters true intimacy. This is the safety of the Focusing relationship. You can receive guidance in forming a Focusing partnership or find a partner by contacting the Focusing Institute. www.focusing.org

A Journaling Guide to Focusing Alone
There will be times when you feel the need to re-connect with yourself but there is no partner available. If you are Focusing alone, I suggest you try a simple journaling technique I often use when I don't have a partner.

Here is my journaling method: I simply write down a few words as I go through the steps. For example, in step one, Clearing a Space, I note down some body sensing words, perhaps tightness in my stomach, and then note whatever it is in my life that seems to be connected to this sensation, whatever comes to mind as I sense into the feeling. Then, I spend a moment or two with whatever it is before putting it on the shelf so that I can return to my body to see what else might be there. I proceed through each step in the same way. For example, when I come to finding a handle, I jot down a few words that seem to fit the feeling until I get to one or two that feel right. Writing down a few words as I go along helps me to stay on track with my process. One of the great ways Focusing helps is by slowing us down so that we can notice all that is going on inside. When it comes to Felt Sensing or resonating I am often tempted to rush through. To compensate for this tendency I spend at least two minutes at each stage. If I hurry the process I miss the depth of all that is there inside.

There are many opportunities to learn more about Focusing. The Focusing Institute provides a list of Focusing teachers and trainers, some of whom you have met in this book. The Institute also has a partnership program in which you can connect with a Focusing partner who is suited to your own level of skill. They first refer you to a teacher who can give you introductory instruction over the phone for a very low fee. As you become more fluent in Focusing you can join a Changes Group.

I hope you will find use for the Focusing method as you continue on your way. The Focusing process is the most direct and simple path to self-discovery that I have ever discovered. The human journey is one of endless potential and limitless growth. The self continues to expand through all the years of life. The key to opening these endless possibilities within you lies in non-judgmental self-exploration. Focusing is a step by step tool that can help you find inner peace, self-acceptance and self-forgiveness.

Biographies

Lucinda Gray, Ph.D
Licensed Psychologist
Coordinator, The Focusing Institute
Lucinda completed her undergraduate work at UCLA, and received her Ph.D. in Clinical Practice from the California School of Professional Psychology in 1977. She first learned Focusing in graduate school and it has been an integral aspect of her approach to psychotherapy. She studied Focusing with Eugene Gendlin, Ph.D. and many other Focusing teachers. For the past thirty years Lucinda has been in private practice as a clinical Psychologist. She consulted in a variety of settings with children, adolescents and adults, and has taught Focusing on all age levels. Most recently she served as Consulting Psychologist to the Centinella Valley Union High School District. She has been teaching workshops in Focusing in the U.S. and internationally, and has presented at numerous conferences all over the world. She is adjunct faculty in Psychology at Santa Barbara Graduate Institute. She is currently completing a new book; **Fast track Meditation - The New Healing Path to Awakening** to be published in 2013. Dr. Gray can be contacted at <www.drlucindagray.com>. She can also be reached by phone in the US at 310-827-4241.

Diana Marder, Ph.D.
Licensed Psychologist
Coordinator, The Focusing Institute
Diana Marder received her Ph.D. in psychology from Harvard University in 1976, and taught at the college level for several years before entering a re-specialization program in clinical psychology. In addition to 19 years in private practice, she has worked with Medi-Cal adult and child recipients and foster children, taught clinical psychology, and supervised interns in an inner city clinic serving the Latin American population. Diana began studying Focusing in 1983 and has been a certified trainer and coordinator with the International Focusing Institute since 2000. She has taught Focusing and Focusing-oriented Psychotherapy in clinical psychology programs, provided in-service training in counseling clinics, private Focusing training workshops and on-going groups. She has been a licensed psychologist since 1989. She has great admiration for school teachers, having decided the job was too difficult for her!
Dr. Marder can be reached at <www.docdiana.com>.

Fernando Hernandez, Ph.D.
Senior Research Fellow
Institute for Computing in the Humanities, Arts and Social Sciences
University of Illinois, Urbana-Champaign
Professor Emeritus, Cal State University Los Angeles
Certified Trainer the Focusing Institute
Dr. Fernando Hernandez is Professor Emeritus at California State University, Los Angeles, where he served as Assistant Dean of Education, Chairman of the Division of Educational Foundations and Interdivisional and as Professor of Education and Professor of Computer Science. He has extensive in experience in the field of Human Development and teaches courses in Educational Psychology, Human Development, Research Methods in Education, Seminar in Advanced Human Development as well as courses in Educational Computing. He holds a PhD in Human Behavior and has taught and done research in both the United States and Latin America. He is currently conducting research and policy work with the Advanced Research and Technology Collaboration for the Americas (ARTCA). This project is funded by the Costa Rica – USA Foundation.

Dr. Hernandez served as an officer in the United States Naval Reserve, from which he recently retired with the rank of Captain (06) after 25 years. In that capacity he saw service aboard the USS Racine, US Navy Recruiting, and served as Executive Officer of the Mobile Inshore, Undersea Warfare Unit. He also has served in the Pentagon for the Undersecretary of the Navy, in the area of Manpower policy and assessment. He also deployed as a Program for Afloat

College Education (PACE) Professor aboard the aircraft carrier USS Kitty Hawk, teaching introductory psychology to sailors that were working on their college degrees while deployed in the Western Pacific.

He is coauthor of a recent book with Steven Valdivia entitled *Forces: From Gangs to Riots,* published by Lulu press: www.lulu.com.
As a psychologist he has a deep interest in human development. He is a certified Trainer with the Focusing Institute.
Dr. Hernandez can be reached at:
fhernan@illinois.edu
Twitter:hernandz_ichass
562 726-4122 messages

Doralee Grindler Katonah, Psy.D., M.Div., Woodland, California
Dr Grindler Katonah is Associate Professor at The Institute of Transpersonal Psychology, Palo Alto, CA. She was the founding director of The Focusing Institute and is a Certifying Coordinator. She is a health psychologist and a practitioner of Zen Buddhism.

Dr. Grindler Katonah can be reached at email: dgk@livingforwardwhole.com
        website: www.livingfowardwhole.com

Mary Hendricks, Ph.D., New York
Mary Hendricks, Ph.D., Director of The Focusing Institute, conducts a private practice as a psychologist. She publishes lectures and teaches workshops worldwide.

Dr. Hendricks can be reached at
The Focusing Institute
info@focusing.org

James Iberg, Ph.D. Chicago, Illinois
I've been practicing Focusing-oriented psychotherapy (E.T. Gendlin, 1996) as a psychologist since 1980, shortly after completing my Ph.D. at the University of Chicago. I have done Focusing training both in the U.S. and internationally, and I am a certifying coordinator for the Focusing Institute, so that I can bring people to a level of expertise with Focusing that gets them certified as Focusing trainers by the Institute. But most of my time is spent in therapy with individuals and couples, and some families, combining my expertise with Focusing with a lot of empathy. I work to create a safe space within which you can open up to the subtleties and nuances of your own feelings.

I also have an M.B.A. from the University of Chicago, so I am very comfortable working with people in business who seek to improve their decision-making, make changes in the course of their careers, improve working relationships, or deal more effectively with difficult fellow employees.

James Iberg, Ph.D. can be reached at his Evanston and Chicago Michigan Avenue Offices
And at www.empathywork.com
847-864-0303

Joan Klagsbrun, Ph.D,, Boston Massachusetts USA .Joan Klagsbrun, Ph.D. is a licensed clinical psychologist in private practice in the Boston area. She has served for decades on the faculty of Lesley University in Cambridge, Massachusetts in the Graduate Counseling Psychology Division, specializing in Holistic and Health Psychology. She has also been an adjunct faculty member at Andover/Newton Theological School.

Dr. Klagsbrun has been teaching Focusing nationally and internationally to psychotherapists, educators, healthcare providers and the public for almost 34 years. She is a Focusing Coordinator in the Boston area, where she teaches and supervises Focusing-oriented psychotherapists. She is a board member of the Focusing Institute as well as the Institute for Body, Mind and Spirituality at Lesley University. Her articles on Focusing in Education have been published in The Folio and The (online) Journal for Pedagogy, Pluralism and Practice.

Dr.Klagsbrun can be reached at joanklag@aol.com or at her website
www.newenglandfocusing.com   Phone 617 924 8515.

Nada Lou—Montreal, Canada
My involvement with Focusing touches on the overlapping qualities of several fascinating fields. A teacher by profession, developing Focusing, TAE and Philosophy courses is an exciting, timely growth in my professional life; As an artistic communicator, I am enthusiastic about the production of Focusing-related DVDs. Immersing myself in Gendlin's thinking, my teaching opened out into the world. After co-presenting TAE with Dr. Gendlin, I took my teaching around the world to North, Central and South America, Australia, New Zealand, China, Hong Kong, Japan and Europe; I authored "Grassroots Introduction Manual to TAE" as a tool for people who are interested in developing this practice; As a Coordinator, I am involved in launching FISS (Focusing Institute Summer School) 5 years ago. I also train Focusing/TAE and Trainers who wish to become Coordinators.

Nada Lou can be contacted at her web site nadalou@nadalou.com

Many clips of Nada's videos are accessible on
YouTube: http://www.focusing.org/multimedia/index.htm.

Kathy McGuire Ph.D., Rogers Arkansas, USA
Dr. Kathy McGuire received the Ph.D. from University of Chicago, working directly with Dr. Eugene Gendlin, creator of Focusing (*Focusing*, Bantam, 1981, 1984). She has had a thirty-five year career as a psychotherapist and workshop leader and Certifying Coordinator for Gendlin's Focusing Institute. She is the director of Creative Edge Focusing(TM).
Creative Edge Focusing ™ represents Dr. McGuire's unique emphasis upon the interpersonal aspects of Listening and Focusing as exemplified in her manual *Focusing In Community: How To Start A Listening/Focusing Support group* (*Focusing en Comunidad* en espanol).

Dr. McGuire is located in Rogers, AR, where she offers coaching for individuals by phone and consultation to organizations and communities.
kathy@cefocusing.com, www.cefocusing.com

Edwin M. McMahon, Ph.D. & Peter A. Campbell, Ph.D.
Sonora California
Edwin M. McMahon, Ph.D. and Peter A. Campbell, Ph.D. are teachers, authors, theologians, Catholic priests and cofounders of The Institute for BioSpiritual Research, Inc. P. O. box 741137, Arvada, Colorado 80006 -- 1137; telephone/fax 303 - 4 2 7 – 5311. E-mail: LFLOM@mho.net or visit our website at: www.BioSpiritual.org.

They are the authors of many books, videos and booklets. Their work is based upon 50 years of psychological research into the body's consciousness and human wholeness.

Drs. McMahon and Campbell have found that once parents, child caregivers, teachers and others who interact with children can personally experience the body-feel of an inner process at work within their own body's language, they are better able to guide children into developing *the habit of noticing and nurturing their own feelings*. This helps children to be more open to learn from all their feelings, instead of cutting themselves off from this essential inner communication necessary for healthy human development and peace-filled societies.

Edwin M. McMahon, Ph.D. and Peter A. Campbell, Ph.D. can be contacted through their website: ***http://www.biospiritual.org***
Or via email at <pcampbel@inreach.com> (N.B. only one "L" in Campbel)
US tel: 209-694-8667

Barbara Merkur, M.A., Toronto Canada
Barbara is a certifying coordinator of the Focusing Institute. At her Centre for Creating Meaning, in Toronto, Canada, she offers Focusing classes and psychotherapy services. Her programs help people express themselves, improve their relationships, subdue their perfectionism and self-criticism, and improve self-image. One of her most successful programs has been with high school students where she engaged them in learning more about themselves through expressive arts therapies techniques. At the Toronto Art Therapy Institute for the past fifteen years she offers a 'Making Art that Moves you' class, where she combines Focusing listening and spontaneous art to help her trainees facilitate change with their practicum clients. She has created many innovative protocols for self discovery such as Focusing Frames (presently being prepared for publication).

Barbara Merkur can be reached at bmerkur66@hotmail.com, or at her office address of 2200 Yonge Street #1302, Toronto, M4S 2C6, (ph. 416-322-7999) and is available for consultation and phone sessions.

Ann Weiser Cornell, Ph.D., Berkeley California
Ann Weiser Cornell is the author of *The Power of Focusing* and *The Radical Acceptance of Everything*, and co-author of *The Focusing Student's and Companion's Manual.* She is located in Berkeley, CA, and teaches over fifty Focusing seminars a year, primarily by phone.

Ann Weiser Cornell is accessible from anywhere. www.focusingresources.com 1-866-720-6106

Lesley Wilson and Addie Van der Kooij, Wiltshire UK
Lesley Wilson and Addie Van der Kooij live in Marlborough, Wiltshire, in the southwest of England. They have been on a journey of spiritual exploration now for over 20 years and Focusing is very much part of this journey for them. They offer Focusing workshops in BioSpiritual Focusing and Wholebody Focusing.

Lesley is a member of the British Focusing Teachers Association and has been teaching BioSpiritual Focusing for 15 years. She coordinates the BioSpiritual Focusing Association in UK which is closely connected to the Institute for BioSpiritual Research www.biospiritual.org

Addie Van der Kooij is a Dutch national and has recently become a Focusing Institute Certified Trainer in WholeBody Focusing. He has worked closely with Kevin McEvenue in exploring, developing and teaching WBF in UK and is co-author of their self-help learning program "Focusing with Your Whole Body".

Addie can be contacted at avdkooy@talktalk.net
Lesley can be contacted at lwilsonBSFA@talktalk.net